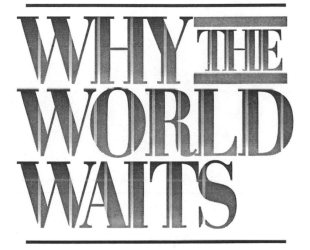

WHY THE WORLD WAITS

Jesus said,
"Say not ye, There are yet four months,
and then cometh harvest?
Behold, I say unto you,
Lift up your eyes, and look on the fields;
for they are white already to harvest....
Pray ye therefore the Lord of the harvest,
that he will send forth labourers into his harvest."
(John 4:35; Matt. 9:38)

K.P. YOHANNAN

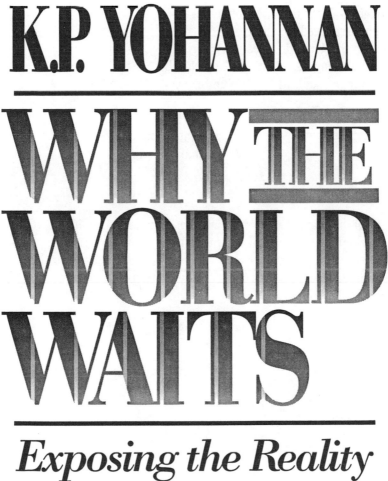

WHY THE WORLD WAITS

Exposing the Reality of Modern Missions

Creation House

Lake Mary, Florida

Copyright © 1991 by K.P. Yohannan
All rights reserved
Printed in the United States of America
Library of Congress Catalog Card Number: 90-82479
International Standard Book Number: 0-88419-303-9

Creation House
Strang Communications Co.
600 Rinehart Road
Lake Mary, FL 32746
(407) 333-0600

Unless otherwise noted, all Scripture quotations are from the King James Version of the Bible.

This book is dedicated to my mother, Achyamma K. Punnose.
On August 27, 1990, she went to be with the Lord.
She was 84. For three and a half years, every Friday,
she fasted and prayed. Her request:
"Lord, please call one of my children to be a missionary."
The Lord answered her prayer. He called me to serve Him.

Acknowledgments

My deepest thanks to:

Robert Walker — for your love for the lost, which is so evident through your excellent editorial work.

Murray at Creation House — for believing in what we do.

Bill — for your help in gathering information and for your most valuable suggestions.

My staff at the GFA international headquarters, USA — what would I do without your encouragement and support? You are the best.

Heidi, my secretary — for your hard work, patiently reading through the manuscript and working endless hours to make it ready for the publisher.

Gisela, my wife, and my children, Daniel and Sarah — my most precious gifts from the Lord. Your love and sacrifice made this book a reality.

K.P. Yohannan
Carrollton, Texas
March 1991

Contents

Preface

Sitting around a folding table in this huge old Dallas church building was a small group of remarkable people. They were, and still are, some of the most sincere Christian men and women you could ever meet. They gather once a month, bringing along their brown bag lunches, to talk about the thing they love the most — foreign missions.

They represent many different backgrounds, both in their secular careers and Christian traditions. But they all share two common denominators. First, they personally sacrifice for missions, supporting the global outreach of the church with prayer and finances. Second, everyone at the table is a local church leader. Most serve as chairpersons of their congregations' missions committees.

This is a sober, serious-minded group. Each plays an important role in determining the budget and helping to raise the funds to support his or her church's foreign missions budget.

Men and Women Behind the Scenes

As a missions leader, I knew these men and women were very typical of the few thousand North American leaders who have directed over $1.9 billion annually into overseas missions. Because of their support, over 75,167 U.S. and Canadian missionaries currently are stationed around the world, according to John Siewert, co-editor of *Mission Handbook* from Missions Advanced Research Center.[1]

Many in the room had visited the mission field, and all had heard scores of missionary speakers over the years. Some of them were pastors or had been missionaries. All had close friends, fellow church members or even relatives who were serving overseas as American missionaries. Many acted as full- or part-time local representatives for their favorite missionary board or cause.

These are the ones who "tarried by the stuff" and were promised their equal share in the victory by King David in 1 Samuel 30:24. Without men and women like these, the Great Commission enterprise of the Western church would find it difficult to survive.

I had been invited to meet with this group, not so much as a speaker, but to answer their questions about the rapid growth of the native missionary movement. I had been specifically asked to represent the views of indigenous mission leaders from the Third World.

Most of them already had a copy of my first book, *The Coming Revolution in World Missions*, and I came to the meeting prepared to defend my convictions and answer tough questions.

Already Convinced About Native Missions

I was shocked when, after I finished a short introduction to our ministry, one of the men stood to his feet and spoke.

"Brother K.P.," he said, "we already know that indigenous missions are now the key to the future of missions. We want to be part of what God is doing. The critical things you have to say about our programs are shocking, but we all know they're true.

"I wish everyone in my church could hear what you have to say. None of us opposes native missionaries. We just don't know how we can best help. And we need to know how to answer the questions of others when we try to explain to them what's happening on the field. Tell us how to build a case for native missionary support in our churches, and we'll do it."

His challenge took me a little by surprise. For over a decade traditional missions thinking in the United States and Europe has broken my heart. The increasingly tragic waste of energy, finances and time continues to trouble me.

Here was a group of respected local missions leaders struggling with the same problem!

"Well," I asked carefully, "what kind of questions are you getting from your people and leaders?"

For the next two hours we talked back and forth. The questions they raised were uncommonly candid. I answered them as boldly and frankly as I could:

• How can we spot authentic missionaries and know that our support is making a real difference for Christ?

• What's really happening on the mission field? Are there qualified indigenous missionaries ready to be supported?

• Why aren't Western missionaries effective in so many nations of the world?

• Why are so many nations closing their doors to Western missions and missionaries?

• What role should Western Christians and churches play in the Third World today?

• Is there a good ratio between Western and indigenous missionaries on the field? What should it be?

• How do we evaluate the work of native missionaries?

• How can you hold indigenous missionaries accountable?

• How much does it cost to support native missionaries, and at what standard of living should missionaries live?

• Do Third World leaders want only Western dollars and nothing else from us?

• Should Western missions be subordinate to native leadership on the field?

• Why does it take our Western missionaries so long to disciple local believers and plant indigenous churches?

• If what you say is true, how can we change the national policies of our churches and denominations?

As the ideas bounced back and forth, I realized these were legitimate questions every Christian leader in the West should be asking. And I also realized I knew of no guidebook available to give these key men and women the answers they needed.

Unity in the Cause of World Evangelism

How will we be able to mobilize the whole church to go to the unreached peoples unless leaders like these have the answers they need? I have realized for years that only as Christians work together in unity on an international level will we ever finish the job. But to accomplish that unity, we must provide Western Christians the up-to-date facts about what is really happening on the mission field today.

For years we've talked about a revolution in world missions, but during that meeting I realized afresh that church leaders in the West still have a key role to play in completing this revolution.

The fact is that God has made us codependent on one another, in the positive sense of the word. As the universal body of Christ, we will not finish the harvest until sending churches in Western nations join hands with indigenous missions to commission more reapers.

So that's how this book came about.

Western leadership needs answers to questions about the way native missions relate to doctrine, history, theology and missions policy. Without these facts they cannot define the cause of native missions intelligently and motivate action. While I don't pretend to be a scholar, these are the areas I want to address from hands-on experience.

This book is designed to give some practical answers that will help church leaders deal with what may be the next great move of the Holy Spirit for world evangelism — a move that will call upon the whole church to unite in the work ahead of us.

Time for Telling the Truth

I have tried to make this a truly honest book about missions policy — one that communicates what thousands of Third World church leaders would like to say to the sending churches in the West if only they could.

Everywhere I speak and travel in the West I sit down with earnest pastors and church leaders who want desperately to move with the Holy Spirit. They sense that something exciting and wonderful is happening today in world evangelism, and they want to be part of what God is doing.

These are the kinds of leaders who will, I trust, find in the following pages the answers for which they've been praying.

K.P. Yohannan
Carrollton, Texas
March 1991

Notes

[1]W. Dayton Robert and John A. Siewert, eds., *Mission Handbook: USA/Canada Protestant Ministries Overseas — 14th Edition* (Grand Rapids, Mich.: Zondervan Publishing House, 1989), pp. 51, 66.

Introduction

Every reader should understand some qualifications about the contents of this book.

First, I am dealing primarily with the unreached countries of the world where Western missionaries are unable to go. There are exceptions to every assertion about to be made. Certainly not everything applies to all mission groups at all times and in all places. (I am thinking especially of the open door God has given Western missionaries in the Eastern European countries.) Different missions are experiencing the natural evolution in colonial missionary policy at different rates. This book must report general trends, and we recognize there are those who will take exception to some of the ideas about to be expressed.

Second, this book is primarily a cry to the churches of the West, an invitation to believers to participate with us in what the Holy Spirit is already doing through native missions today. This is not meant to be a debaters' handbook of academic missions theory. I hope missiologists accept this book as an added voice from Third World leadership, but I am not attempting to join in Western scholarly debate.

Any reader who uses this message to divide the body of Christ, sit in judgment on others or remain uncommitted to the Great Commission task will have missed the point entirely.

Third, although this book calls for policy reviews and changes in obsolete strategy, it is not an attack on any existing group or movement. There are many beneficial and excellent outreach ministries which I believe are outside the scope of the Great Commission mandate. They are an important part of the Christian's personal and corporate life. This book is not intended to be an attack on compassionate ministries, family ministries or social-justice ministries per se.

Checking Our Priorities

These ministries and many like them often are valuable. However, we cannot stand by and let them be substituted for the basic priorities of the Great Commission. The greatest enemy of the *best* is not the worst — but the *good*. And this is exactly what has often happened in Western missions today. Our programs are filled with many good things that have kept us from fulfilling His best!

In a word, that is what this book is meant to be all about — setting priorities. It is time for the church in the West to reset them. We must let Christ's passion for the lost direct our agendas, budgets, goals and schedules. It is time to question priorities which have been set for the church by popular culture, education, entertainment, media and theology.

God has not called the church as an institution to market, farm, govern, manufacture, trade or police this world, but to preach and teach all that Christ taught us.

This book is a cry for the next generation of Christians to act. In the 1990s we must see the reformation of much of Western missions. Only such a reformation will enable us in the Third World to complete the Great Commission mandate in our generation.

If this book does a bit to turn us back to our first purposes, it will be worth the tears and pain that went into every page. Discipline is never pleasant for the moment, but in the end it brings the godliness and righteousness that we all desire to see in the house of God. This is a challenge that must be made if we are to fulfill the passion of Christ for this lost and dying world.

Book I

———————————— 1 ————————————

End of an Era

The year was 1939, only yesterday in comparison to the history of the church and Christian missions. Although no one imagined it a half-century ago, the curtain was about to fall on over five hundred years of empire and colonial rule by the West.

In Europe, Hitler was about to launch a war against the last of the great colonial powers. It was a struggle that would clamp Britain and her North Atlantic allies into a nearly fatal choke hold. Meanwhile, taking advantage of the situation in Asia, the warlords of Japan were preparing to launch a war that would forever break the Western grip on the Orient.

After World War II the bankrupt and exhausted colonial powers would have neither the will nor the stamina to resist the rising tide of nationalism and the Marxist communism that fueled it. It swept the world with intense fury. The United Nations records the birth of over one hundred new nation states in the three decades that followed.

For church historians 1939 also marks the end of what is now fondly referred to as "The Great Century" in Christian missions.[1]

It was under the so-called armies of colonial occupation — explorers, traders, exploiters — sent mostly from the Anglo-Saxon countries of Europe, that missionaries like William Carey and Hudson Taylor planted the seeds of evangelical Christianity worldwide. Their nineteenth-century followers managed in only about seventy-five years of actual ministry to foster indigenous church movements on all the major mission fields of Africa, Asia and Latin America.

These were the days when missionaries went overseas on one-way tickets, fully aware they might never see family and home churches again. For thousands, the decision was indeed a fatal one — for themselves and their wives and children. Their graves today dot every great mission field. These pioneers considered the cost, and they gladly laid down their lives to plant the seeds of the gospel in barren fields which today are mature and ready to harvest.

These missionaries demonstrated the true servant spirit of Jesus, loving the people God called them to and faithfully preaching the Word of God.

At the same time there were also many problems. Some nearly fatal mistakes were made at the beginning, stemming mostly from the early "compound strategies" adapted from Spanish Catholic missions to Latin America. Nearly all Protestant mission boards experimented with some form of compound evangelism, and many maintained them well into the twentieth century in modified forms.

Compounds were often the only option in situations where security and treaty restrictions required them. Unfortunately, many missionary societies came to consider them standard operating procedure. Required or not, there is no doubt they were the preferred method to maintain an island of safety in the midst of an often violent environment.

These compounds in their original form were something like self-sustaining Christian forts. Converts, who were frequently disowned by family and community, sought shelter in these centers and thus were isolated from the rest of their native society. Many worked in agricultural, educational and medical projects that were developed around the compounds. Unfortunately, while they learned the Christian faith, they also learned alien cultures and technologies which separated them even further from family, friends and non-Christian neighbors.

But despite these early experiments in witness by segregation, the Lord used the lives of these pioneers to make genuine disciples. Soon, truly indigenous churches emerged within one local culture after another. The power of the gospel was released through native witness, and today there are thriving local churches on nearly all mission fields as a result.

Along with indigenous churches have come indigenous mission boards, gospel teams and evangelistic societies. In fact, at this time the number of these native missionaries is growing five times faster than missionaries sent from the West. On many mission fields native missionaries already outnumber their Western colleagues, some authorities say, and will surpass them on a worldwide basis sometime in 1998.[2]

At the time of this writing, Gospel for Asia supported well over six thousand native missionaries in India alone. But it is not uncommon to read reports in Western publications that list the number of native missionaries in India anywhere from only four hundred to three thousand. Plainly, the correct size of the native missionary force is not being reported accurately. In an interview for this book, one agency cooperating with native missionaries actually asserted that by their reckoning the number of native missionaries worldwide already exceeds traditional missionaries by about 125,000.

In this sense the work of colonial missions was an unqualified success. These men and women laid down their lives, and as a result the Holy Spirit is now calling out an army of indigenous missionaries who are the products of their witness to finish the Great Commission task. Volumes have been filled with the adventures and sacrifices of these pioneer missionaries from America and Europe. They left footprints of suffering on the pages of history which few in the West would even consider following today.

But the self-sacrifice and heroism of these nineteenth-century missionaries have an entirely different interpretation in the secular history books of emerging Third World nations. There, faith in Christ is seldom described in biblical or Western terms. It is not seen as a personal choice each individual must make before God.

Missions and Cultural Imperialism

The gospel and its proclamation by white foreigners are portrayed as a sinister form of imperialism. Christian missions are usually linked to every injustice or sinful exploitation of native peoples during the colonial era. Critics often portray evangelism as *the most subtle* and dangerous incursion of Western imperialism on local society because, they say, it appears so benign. Although the gospel is admitted to be nonpolitical, nonmilitary and noneconomic, this is the very reason it is considered the most dangerous alien influence of all. In fact, the Bible itself also remains one of the most feared and hated books in most Third World countries — especially those which have embraced Marxist or Islamic social orders.

Unfortunately, there is more than a grain of truth in some of these criticisms. During the colonial era some misguided missionaries encouraged Christian converts to change their names, manner of dress and life-styles to conform to that of the "civilized West." Conversion to Christ too often meant an informal adaptation of foreign cultural baggage and occidental prejudices as well. Occasionally during the colonial era some converted to Christianity for economic reasons or to gain favor with the ruling elite.

Bruce Britten, veteran missionary to Swaziland, explains how this took place in Africa: "Some problems have resulted from the fact that most African nations have received Christianity from Europeans instead of receiving it from Ethiopians or other North African Christians. Probably the main problem is that Christianity in most of Africa is now mixed with European customs. Of course, this is because the European missionaries who came to Africa brought not only the Christian faith, but they also brought their own customs.

"Naturally, it was difficult for the people of Africa to see the difference between the Christian faith and European customs. In fact, the missionaries themselves had difficulty seeing which things really belonged to the Christian faith and which things were just their own customs. The result was that Christianity and European customs became so mixed up that the European way of singing seemed to be the *Christian* way of singing, European musical instruments seemed to be the *Christian* instruments, and European clothes seemed to be *Christian* clothes. Therefore, most of the Africans who accepted Christianity also accepted all the European customs.

"Often an African was not accepted as a true Christian unless he agreed to throw away his own culture and conform to European culture."[3]

It takes a miracle for most Westerners, particularly Americans, to comprehend how bitterly humiliating this colonial period was to the once-proud peoples of Africa, Asia and the Middle East. Words cannot overstate or exaggerate how deeply the Christian religion and colonial exploitation remain linked as one in the minds of countless millions.

Only as we consider the anti Western fanaticism of the late Ayatollah Khomeini in Iran, Ho Chi Minh in Vietnam and Mao Tse-tung in China do we begin to understand the hatred resulting from colonialism.

Unforgiveness Lingers

Most missionaries from the West cannot help but be aware of this lingering unforgiveness felt by so many — and the barrier it creates to evangelism. Though they have tried various social programs to bridge the gap, Western missionaries today often find themselves still unable to restore a credible Christian testimony. Therefore, with the exception of a few one-on-one contacts, many Western missionaries have retreated from open evangelistic work and direct church planting.

What can happen when a Western missionary recognizes his need to identify with the national is illustrated in an account by former missionary doctor Arden Almquist, executive secretary of World Missions of the Evangelical Covenant Church of America. He served in the Congo (now Zaire) when the country was under Belgian rule. He shares some of his first impressions as a new missionary:

"I was struck at once by the sharp contrast between the splendor of the European sector — greater than that known by most Belgians in Brussels or Antwerp — and the relative squalor of the African sector....

"Eating was largely a segregated function, except on rare occasions. Not only was it unusual for an African to be seated at a white man's table; white men, including missionaries, rarely ate at an African's.

"I was giving the grand tour of the Wasolo mission one day to a visiting Norwegian missionary. It was mid-afternoon, and the mission workmen were seated outside their huts after having their daily bath following the cessation of the day's work. They were drinking coffee as we walked by, and they offered my guest and me a cup. I accepted mine, served in a glass, very black, and almost syrupy from too much sugar. My friend refused with a '*Non, merci!*' then turned to me, saying in English: 'Surely you don't drink with these people? Aren't you concerned about getting dysentery?'

"But it was not only fear that handicapped the missionary. There was a kind of conspiracy of solidarity of race and culture that made him insensitive to his own basic humanity.

"Christmas was an example. For weeks before and after Christmas the large SoTransCongo truck which tripled as a commercial carrier, local bus and mail wagon made its weekly stop at the Karawa post, disgorging each time a dozen sacks of mail, filled with parcels from the States — gifts for the missionaries and their 'benighted' children whom the thoughtful donors imagined to be so exposed to the hazards of jungle life; and so cheated of the gimmicks of an ever-expanding affluent American society. For the African 'boy' or nurse or teacher or pastor there were no gifts — they had no relatives overseas. There was tacit agreement among the missionaries — indeed at one time a station council ruling — that no individual missionary was to give a Christmas present to an African individual. Instead there was a Christmas party by the missionaries as a group for the Africans as a group.

"This conspiracy of solidarity included the nonmissionary members of the white race, the Belgians, Portuguese, and Greeks who made up the white community. Whatever their personal qualities or qualifications, or lack of them, they were recognized as 'belonging' in a special way, although many of them showed little or no evidence of faith in Christ. Gradually, as the days became months, and the months years, one got caught up in these attitudes.

"There was a conspiracy of solidarity in the African community too, as rigid as our own, as an experience toward the close of my first term of four years made clear.

"We had a strike at the Wasolo station. It began when I dismissed five student nurses. Quickly the solidarity of the African community manifested itself. The workmen quit working, and all building ceased. The schoolteachers sent the two hundred pupils home. Work at the hospital came to a standstill. It was my fault — I had injured the Africans' keen sense of justice in a burst of anger. It was easy to rationalize my deed. Four of the five had stolen medications, or accepted bribes for services, or been delinquent on duty. I had warned them, but to no avail. In exasperation I had summarily dismissed the class and told them to return to their villages. But I had done so in anger, and I had been unfair to one among the five whom everyone felt to be innocent. I talked it over with the senior missionary on the station, who smiled awkwardly and told me: 'It's your problem. You got yourself into it. You'll have to handle it.'

"I returned to my room to pray together with my wife. Then, humbled, I took a can of powdered coffee and some sacks of sugar and went down to the African village where the strikers, in a sullen mood, were sitting around their small fires in front of their huts. I told them I was sorry and asked them to forgive me. Then I invited them to add hot water from their cooking pots to the symbols of reconciliation in my hands, so that we might share a cup of coffee together and talk things over. They listened in silence, with growing interest. There were murmurs of surprise and suddenly there was joy! We shook hands all around and drank together. I agreed to review my hasty decision, and they agreed to return to work and recall the schoolchildren to their classes. There were tears and laughter, and someone said: 'Doctor, this is the first time a white man ever apologized to us.' "[4]

New Third World Leaders React

Moreover, Third World leaders cannot forget that many of their former colonial masters openly ridiculed local culture, language, religion and history. Furthermore, they blame their current economic, military and technological dependence on centuries of exploitation by the so-called Christian empires of Britain, France, Holland, Spain and Portugal. American military adventures in Latin America, Southeast Asia and the Middle East since World War II have further prejudiced many.

Today, although the revolutionary zeal of nationalism may be fading, a new generation of Third World leaders continues to act out this inherited bitterness. Restrictions on missionary activity by foreigners is one of the easiest and most popular ways to strike back.

In *China*, foreign missionaries are still banned by the Chinese forty years after the communist revolution. Despite token Bible printings, it remains almost impossible to obtain the Scriptures in China today. China's population will reach 1.2 billion by A.D. 2000 — and worldwide over 1.5 billion will speak Chinese. With two thousand unreached people groups, China represents the largest single concentration of unevangelized people in the world. Yet there is no sign that it will open soon to Western missionary evangelists and church planters.[5]

In modern *Africa* there is an almost universal wall against Western evangelistic missionaries. The newly independent nations of Africa are demanding that Western missionaries bring humanitarian and secular skills into the economy. If missionaries cannot justify their presence in the cause of nation-building, visas will not be granted. Yet over eight hundred unreached people groups still remain in Africa.[6]

In *Myanmar*, known for centuries as Burma, Christian missionaries from the West are banned despite the fact that mission hospitals and schools were the primary sources of social services in the nation until 1960. Myanmar, once one of the richest and most progressive nations in the Third World, is today not only among the poorest but is actually going back in time to an era without modern medicine or education. Yet Myanmar's nationalistic leaders apparently still prefer present conditions to the possibility of opening their doors to Christian missionaries from the outside.

Myanmar's anti-Christian and anti-Western prejudice is shared by most Asian nations from Afghanistan to Vietnam.

Around the world and especially in the *Middle East*, nations with over 50 percent Muslim majorities have almost universally banned missionaries since their independence. Shiite fundamentalists and other conservative groups are pressuring for a return to Koranic laws which call for Jihad, or "holy wars," against America, a nation they portray as "the great Satan" for spreading immorality in Islamic nations.

Conversion to Christianity remains a capital offense in many Muslim nations, and those who turn to Jesus Christ are cut off from family, friends and society.

Islamic fundamentalists and other reactionaries have introduced restrictive legislation against Western missionaries in thirty-one countries, according to J. Dudley Woodberry, a respected authority on Islam. These nations include: *North Africa* — Algeria, Egypt, Libya, Morocco, Sudan and Tunisia; *West Africa* — Mauritania; *East Africa* — Comoros, Djibouti and Somalia; *West Asia* — Bahrain, Iraq, Jordan, Kuwait, Lebanon, Oman, Qatar, Saudi Arabia, Syria, Turkey, United Arab Emirates and Yemen; *South Asia* — Afghanistan, Bangladesh, Iran, Maldives and Pakistan; *Southeast Asia* — Brunei, Indonesia and Malaysia.[7]

By A.D. 2000 1.2 billion people will be Muslims if the present annual increase continues at 2.7 percent. Today there are 908 million Muslims worldwide with 4,000 separate unreached people groups![8]

Yet current relations between Muslim countries and the West seem to be worsening rather than improving, making the atmosphere for Western missionaries more difficult than ever.

Since 1947 these rising tides of Third World nationalism have made strange bedfellows. In government and education they have adopted secular humanistic systems of thought and economics, including subtle forms of Marxism and Leninism. A near worship of science and technology also prevails. On the spiritual level, nationalism has helped to foster revivals of primitive religions.

Notes

[1]Ruth A. Tucker, *From Jerusalem to Irian Jaya* (Grand Rapids, Mich.: Zondervan Publishing House, 1983), p. 109.

[2]Larry D. Pate, *From Every People* (Monrovia, Calif.: MARC, 1989), pp. 51, 54.

[3]Bruce Britten, *We Don't Want Your White Religion* (Manzini, Swaziland, 1984), p. 25.

[4]Arden Almquist, *Missionary, Come Back!* (Cleveland, Ohio: World Publishing, 1970), pp. 4-14.

[5]Allan Starlin, *Seeds of Promise* (Pasadena, Calif.: William Carey Library, 1981), p. 94.

[6]*Ibid.*

[7]Unpublished study paper by David B. Barrett, *Global Statistics Summary* (Manila, Philippines: Lausanne II Congress on World Evangelization Statistical Task Force, July 11-20, 1989).

[8]Starlin, *Seeds of Promise*, p. 94.

Restrictions:
Bane of Missions Today

The impact of the anti-Western movement among the Third World family of nations has been devastating.

Before *perestroika and the sweeping changes in Eastern Europe, at least 119 nations prohibited or restricted Western missionaries, and an average of four new countries were being added to the list each year. Currently 3.8 billion people live in these restricted-access countries, and 4.8 billion will live in them by the turn of this century.*[1]

It is too soon to tell what impact the relaxed cold war restrictions on the church in the Soviet world will have on missionary activity. However, to date, *glasnost* and *perestroika have still not opened the doors to traditional missions.*

If present trends continue, by A.D. 2000 over 77 percent of the entire world population could live in nations closed to identifiable missionaries from Western countries.[2]

Only in Latin America, it seems, have most nations failed to restrict Western missionaries solely on the basis of a nationalistic reaction. Yet Marxism in Cuba and the revolution in Central America have been flavored with a strong anti-missionary and anti-clerical fervor. Liberation theology is a sworn enemy to traditional evangelism, and most Latin American nations have documented harassment and persecution of missionaries.

Even Mexico, America's closest neighbor to the south, forbids traditional missionaries to cross its borders.

Western missionaries who have remained overseas in this atmosphere have generally found their attempts at evangelism increasingly difficult. Nationalism has created a xenophobia in which white evangelists are viewed as foreign agents. In fact, even in the more open nations such as Brazil, Colombia or Nigeria, it can be difficult for a Western missionary to do public work without accusations of being "American CIA."

White missionaries in many countries must deal with anger, bitterness or polite indifference based on the past sins of their nations.

In his exploration of African resistance to the gospel, Bruce Britten asks this question: "Why is it that many Africans today feel they don't want anything 'white'? The answer is obvious. While everyone agrees that not all whites are the same, the fact remains that for hundreds of years many whites have looked down on and oppressed the people of Africa. It would be foolish for anyone to deny this."[3]

This reaction is comparable to the resistance white gospel workers sense when they attempt to plant churches among the Sioux Indians of North and South Dakota. Not only are these tribes still immersed in the animistic traditions of native religion, but they are the great-grandchildren of the Indians massacred at Wounded Knee by U.S. cavalry in the late 1800s. Those memories are too fresh.

For most Americans, however, who have never been subjugated by an outside power, these kinds of feelings can be hard to understand. But memories of foreign occupation can be even more deadly. African and Asian nations have their equivalent of KKK "night riders" too.

As this book was being written, missionary hostages were held in Colombia and Lebanon by guerilla leaders whose revolutionary movements are fueled by an intense hatred of the West — and therefore of Western missionaries.

Mission Reactions — Denial, Despair and Defense

Although missionaries returning to the field after World War II intellectually understood they were coming back to a different world, many failed to see how permanent and serious this deep crisis in Western missions really was. The victorious Americans were especially unwilling to accept the coming reality of life in newly independent nations. Instead of working with the rising tides of nationalism, they called for even more Western volunteers, funds and programs!

Meanwhile, however, many secular corporations reacted just the opposite. Sensing the depth of the change in public opinion, they sought alternate ways to manufacture and market their products to Third World customers. The keystone of almost every successful business strategy was to find a way to adapt to nationalism by eliminating or minimizing the physical presence of foreign personnel. Failing that, they tried to maintain operations with the smallest expatriate staff possible.

Western businesses quickly trained local personnel to replace their foreign staff, promoted natives to leadership positions, sought local investors, began joint ventures and licensed their patents to indigenous manufacturers.

But not colonial missions leaders. Many attempted to find ways to stay on, maintain as much control as possible and run their mission compounds as before. They tried to ride out what they viewed as a temporary storm.

One eyewitness of the 1949 Communist takeover of the Shanghai headquarters of one of the best-known agencies (who asked to remain anonymous) reveals a telling anecdote about this widespread attitude. As they packed their bags to leave those beautiful facilities, missionaries joked openly with one another about the impending move.

"We've been through this before," laughed one. "We'll be back!"

For years they waited to return, even keeping the old name intact; meanwhile the Communists turned their Shanghai offices into the local party headquarters! Finally missions executives realized the new anti-missionary rules were here to stay. Eventually they changed their name and moved the work to more open nations which didn't restrict their activities. Ironically, one by one many of these nations have closed their doors also.

In some countries missions were allowed to phase out their operations gradually. Even then many resisted to the end — until the new nationalist governments gave the intransigent ones no other choice. They were simply ordered out. Those who had made disciples and had already

33

turned the control of their ministries over to indigenous churches saw their ministries survive and grow. Those who had not lost everything.

But in those few nations which let missionaries stay, the post-war days presented a new challenge. They had to find new ways to continue on and justify their existence to their hosts. Here are some of the more common strategies used by colonial-style missions to remain on the field after independence.

Carrying on as if nothing had happened. This "business as usual" approach is mostly used by a tiny minority of missionaries who have continued to attempt evangelism and church-planting work. They have chosen to ignore political and social change as much as possible. Some persist in difficult pioneer work, often among tribal and primitive peoples or in urban areas. Most post-colonial nations have denied them visas. In such cases these missionaries are occasionally found in border regions or urban slums, quietly working with concentrations of refugees and students from the main people group they hope to return to sometime in the future.

It is significant that only a small percentage of the North American missionaries working overseas are still engaged in this kind of traditional soul-winning ministry. In fact, the Missions Advanced Research Center in Pasadena has stopped recording statistics on field activities of North American missionary personnel. So many agencies refuse to reply to questions on this subject that collecting valid statistics is no longer possible.

The only official figures from MARC show that a mere 10 percent of the average missionaries from mainline, evangelical churches are involved in evangelism or church planting. Other agencies report 27 percent (the Evangelical Foreign Missions Association), 28 percent (the Interdenominational Foreign Missions Association) and 33 percent (non-associated missions).[4]

But even if we were to agree with the most positive outlook, that 33 percent of all North American missionaries are primarily involved in evangelism and church planting, that still leaves 67 percent in support activities.

Substituting social work. This is by far the most popular substitute for evangelism on the mission field today. Since most Third World nations refuse to welcome foreign evangelists, many missionaries and sending agencies have changed their image in the host country. They now seek to come to the mission field as agricultural and development workers, child-care providers, medical missionaries and teachers.

But fearful that even this humanitarian work will be used as a ruse for evangelism, some nations, such as Nepal, require these missionaries to sign nonproselytizing agreements. Under these contracts missionaries promise not to evangelize or make converts. (This is such an important subject that an entire chapter will be devoted to it.)

The late Donald McGavran, leading church-growth spokesman of the last decade, deplored this trend toward increased emphasis on health, education and economic productivity. "Missiology needs to state clearly that no amount of physical or mental advance outranks spiritual rebirth."[5]

Substituting "pre-evangelism" ministries. In some cases Western missionaries have been allowed to stay and work in tribal areas as anthropologists and linguists doing translation and literacy work. Again, this is frequently permitted only with restrictions or under nonproselytizing contracts with various departments of host governments.

Substituting technical ministries. In other cases missionaries have turned to behind-the-scenes ministries such as becoming audio or video-tape specialists, broadcast producers and technicians, computer programmers, engineers, journalists, mechanics, program managers, pilots and research specialists.

This is a true twilight zone of modern Christian missions. Such ministries are harder to fit into the New Testament pattern of missions for strict literalists. There is no doubt that the aid these specialists provide is increasingly important as mission organizations take advantage of mass media and advanced technology, but it is still not evangelism.

Substituting "fraternal worker" arrangements. Many missions, unwilling to let go of the established churches and denominational structures they founded generations ago, have discovered ways to keep their missionaries in the country as advisers and counselors to the national church. These missionaries often occupy the same mission compounds and enjoy the same privileges their forebears did. (In fact, some of them actually are the grandchildren and great-grandchildren of pioneer missionaries who came to these fields in the last century.)

Imported automobiles and foods, servants, private schools and club memberships often are a way of life for these missionaries — many of whom have now become more a part of the social elite than they were in colonial days. This life of privilege and luxury has built a wall of separation between these missionaries and the people they have come to serve.

Most of these missionaries, because they control strategic foreign funds and have enormous prestige, have in effect become behind-the-scenes executives or program controllers in the national church.

They frequently hold teaching positions at the Bible schools and seminaries which supply clergy to national churches. Through financial grants to hospitals, publishing houses, relief organizations, summer camps and scholarship aid they are able to manipulate and direct the affairs of their so-called indigenous churches.

The tragedy of the career path chosen by these mission leaders is compounded by the fact that their life-styles often are emulated by emerging native leaders. Not only are these missionaries refusing to live the Jesus style of servant leadership themselves, but they are setting an example for indigenous leadership which produces future generations of national leadership that also rules rather than serves the people.

Substituting surrogate missionaries. Some missionaries and the denominations or parachurch organizations they represent have found another approach to remaining on the mission field, which they often describe as "using nationals." Unfortunately, this is an accurate description of what actually takes place.

Similar to the fraternal-worker agreement, this scenario also unfolds when a wealthy mission organization plays the major role. In an effort to portray an image of success, a foreign missionary will recruit local Christians from existing ministries to staff mass evangelism or church programs. In some tragic cases poor native pastors have actually joined a foreign denomination in exchange for a monthly stipend.

These new recruits often are photographed for missionary magazines and public relations at home, thus glamorizing the activity of these national workers and especially the Western missionary behind the scenes.

Though the image of effectiveness and success can be portrayed for a short while, the inevitable results are disastrous on the field. When the attractive compensations which first motivated these native workers peter out, or when their commitment is tested, they often disappear. Second, and most tragic, this type of deception produces all kinds of victims. Nonbelievers in the local community have even more of an excuse to ridicule and refuse God's grace and salvation. As a result the struggling indigenous church is weakened, and — worst of all — un-reached souls remain unreached.

Substituting tentmaking. One of the newest and most publicized responses to Third World nationalism is popularly called "tentmaking." Under this strategy, covert missionaries engage in secular employment and businesses on mission fields which are otherwise closed to foreign missionaries.

Some actually immigrate, giving up their citizenship to marry local citizens and become part of the society in their adopted homelands.

Indeed, there are some successful models of tentmaking today. Yet few of these underground missionaries are establishing living churches.

There is some question whether this new generation of tentmakers should even be considered missionaries. Actually, they are in practice lay Christians who choose to live out their faith in a foreign land and culture.

What influence, if any, this movement will have on the ultimate fulfillment of the Great Commission is yet to be seen. Tentmakers seldom go to the field equipped for the spiritual dangers and trials they will face, nor are they adequately supported by a network of praying friends at home. Since tentmaking is a relatively new phenomenon, statistics on attrition are not yet available in a form that lends itself to comparison.

Using the "my way or else" response. There is one more response to nationalism, which probably would best fit into the *non*response category. It is one of the saddest of all tactics to which some mission organizations have resorted.

In the face of rising native aspirations, some missionaries have left the field, abandoning a ministry or project without transferring the ministry to natives or providing transitional funding.

Two sad examples of this recently occurred in India. A certain colonial-style mission, which is still respected and raising funds in North America, was denied visa renewals for its last American missionary couple.

The couple were actually only token missionaries, mainly left to supervise the work of a fine Bible school with an excellent native staff. The Indian staff members were long ago ready and able to keep the school and its ministry going. Western missionaries were simply no longer needed.

But rather than release the school to the Indian church, the mission board half a world away voted to sell off the property and close the school. The native staff and national pastors involved were not consulted in the matter. The decision was a simple one to the American board: No foreign missionary in charge means no more Bible school.

Replacing that particular school for the language group involved will require an enormous capital investment and years of work by the indigenous church, if it can be replaced at all. This places on the poor, indigenous church an agonizing new investment in order to maintain a training center for pastors.

In another example, one of the grand old colonial-style missions recently ended generations of work in North India. One of the most important services it rendered was the sponsorship of a much-needed radio broadcast in the local language.

However, since it no longer had any foreign missionary in the country, the mission decided to cancel the broadcast — the only radio program reaching over seventy-five million people! There was no attempt to continue sponsoring the broadcast using any one of the dozens of fine native preachers in that state.

Like most similar mission societies, it still maintains rigid policies against helping with the support of native missionaries. Although from an historic perspective these rules might have made sense in the Victorian world, they no longer make any sense given the situation on the mission field today.

The net result for the work of these once-great missions is stagnation and possible slow death. Their bondage to self-imposed legalisms prevents them from being involved in some of the most exciting Christian movements of our day, including evangelism efforts targeting unreached people groups in restricted-access countries.

For the mission which has its eyes fixed on spreading the gospel and planting churches, there are many ways to continue impacting the Third World. But for the mission which still has its focus only on keeping Western personnel assigned overseas, there is little future.

Notes

[1]Unpublished study paper by David B. Barrett, *Global Statistics Summary* (Manila, Philippines: Lausanne II Congress on World Evangelization Statistical Task Force, July 11-20, 1989).

[2]Barrett, *Global Statistics Summary*.

[3]Bruce Britten, *We Don't Want Your White Religion* (Manzini, Swaziland, 1984), p. 30.

[4]Samuel Wilson and John Siewert, eds., *Mission Handbook: North American Protestant Missions Overseas — 13th Edition* (Monrovia, Calif.: MARC, 1986), p. 616.

[5]Article, "Missiology Faces the Lion," by Donald McGavran, *Missiology: An International Review*, Vol. XVII, No. 3, July 1989, pp. 337, 339.

3

What Is the
Spiritual Bottom Line?

Whatever methods they have used to stay on the field in restricted areas, most North American missionaries overseas will agree the results of their labors are limited in terms of numbers won to Christ or churches established. Of course, there are a few spectacular success stories in certain places, but a close examination of these will show a strong indigenous missionary structure.

In reality true church growth and witness on the mission field today are occurring largely within the realm of native missionary work. As will be shown in following chapters, native missionaries more easily understand the local culture and adapt quickly to the environment.

It would be unfair to write the obituary for traditional missions. Although many are no longer accomplishing the Great Commission task as effectively as they once were, they still are supported by the prayers and finances of a large segment of the body of Christ. The regrettable fact is that sentimental attachment of Western believers has blinded them from seeing the need for change.

Yet, astonishingly enough, there may actually be a revival of interest in traditional foreign missions today.

W. Dayton Roberts, introducing the fourteenth edition of the *Mission Handbook*, published in 1989, writes, "Compared to the data of the 13th edition, which appeared at the end of 1986, there are now more missions, more missionaries, more short termers, and more dollars raised for overseas ministries than ever before."[1]

How much of the increase is due to better research or real growth is debatable. But on the surface there appear to be signs of life in the world of traditional Western missions.

For example:

Missionary recruiting efforts continue at a fast pace. During interviews for this book, Inter-Varsity Christian Fellowship reported that the last Urbana convention cost roughly $5.6 million to stage and attracted nearly nineteen thousand students to hear the challenge for missions. Thousands more were spent by hundreds of mission boards and societies to print promotional literature and produce other materials for the convention. Agency representatives traveled from all over the United States to share the vision for their burden with career-minded Christian students.

The Caleb Project, one of the scores of cooperative programs now motivating and mobilizing students into missions, reported that it spent $585,000 in 1988-89 to conduct its activities aimed at twelve hundred aspiring missionaries. The figure does not cover the costs of fielding four traveling teams, sponsored by mission agencies, that challenged another twenty-six thousand Christian students to consider a missionary career in the past year.

I thank God for movements such as the Caleb Project and conferences such as Urbana. We need more of these conferences to be a challenge for world evangelism. However, let us keep in mind that it is what we *do* after we walk out of these conferences that will make the difference in souls saved.

In addition to the hundreds of independent mission boards, societies and religious orders that are recruiting missionaries, nearly every denomination and thousands of local churches are also challenging their best and brightest young people to go out as missionary staff.

Current statistics on the number of schools and seminaries training missionaries are not available in published form. However, judging from numerous interviews with qualified mission leaders, I estimate that there are presently at least four hundred institutions and formal training programs operating in North America.

The cost of this missionary education infrastructure is rarely defined in church and mission budgets. However, one executive officer of a major agency says he believes his mission invests about a quarter of a million dollars in a missionary from the time of acceptance until the completion of the first term of service — a period still considered training time by most missions.[2]

The figure sounds more than reasonable since many missionary educational costs never show in mission budgets. They are borne by the Christian family and friends. A typical missionary educated in the United States, for example, spends four years in college ($60,000); two years in seminary or Bible school ($40,000); one year raising support ($20,000) — none of which shows formally in the mission education process. These numbers double for married couples, of course, so the actual cost of training a missionary family might easily run as high as $450,000 to $500,000.

The tragedy is that many of these missionaries will not go back to the field for a second term. Robert T. Coote, in his introductory essay to the thirteenth edition of the *Mission Handbook*, states, "A major category of resignations is first-term casualties....It is generally thought that up to half of all new missionaries do not last beyond their first term."[3]

In addition, thousands of students will complete missionary training and never go to the field at all. As a result the whole missionary education process indeed appears inefficient. There is more than a little irony involved in the fact that missiology was an unknown academic subject during the halcyon days of Western missions. Yet this year hundreds of formal degrees will be granted in a subject which would seem to have a limited future.

Meanwhile, missions budgets continue to grow year after year. Denominations, mission boards and Christian organizations raised $1.9 billion in 1989 to send North Americans overseas to operate programs for Western church agencies,[4] a growth of 44 percent over the previous four years.

In fact, according to Ralph Winter at the U.S. Center for World Mission, three hundred new North American mission boards have been formed since 1950. Each new edition of the *Mission Handbook* from MARC faithfully records the new mission start-ups, and there is no indication this trend will change.

Now the challenge to complete world evangelization in the next decade is being sounded by many in the old missions system. While we welcome the concept of these A.D. 2000 movements that are currently mapping global strategies for world evangelism, I am certain they could fail if they are imposed on local churches overseas in the same old way, and by the same Western missions.

One only hopes these programs are not manufactured in the flesh, but rather represent a move of the Holy Spirit. David B. Barrett and James W. Reapsome, who authored *Seven Hundred Plans to Evangelize the World*, say they have found over 788 global plans for world evangelism proposed since A.D. 30.[5]

At the Lausanne II Congress on World Evangelization in Manila, held in 1989, more than two thousand plans for evangelism (both global and local) were on the drawing boards for the "Great Commission Decade" ending in A.D. 2000. At the time, seventy-eight of the plans called for budgets exceeding $100 million in U.S. dollars. Thirty-three are planning to spend more than $1 billion for a decade of church growth.[6]

If not of God, these A.D. 2000 programs are simply another attempt at fulfilling God's call with fleshly resources, just as Abraham did in Genesis 16. Unfortunately, this will only produce Ishmaels — never Isaacs.

But if they are of the Lord, we will know them by the way they relate *as servants* to the emerging mission agencies of the Third World. The question is: Will they support and encourage indigenous native missionary movements, or insist on coming in and running more programs on the backs of the nationals?

Why Colonial Missions Perpetuate Themselves

If I were to claim that the Model T Ford was the greatest method of transportation of all time, I doubt anyone would take me seriously. True, in its day the Model T was on the cutting edge of technology. We look admiringly back to this turning point in transportation history, but that day is over. You and I realize this, and we've moved ahead with the times to faster and more efficient ways of getting around.

Unfortunately, many colonial-style mission organizations are still clinging to their "Model T's," holding up traditional mission methods as the best and (often) only way to reach the world. But what is the reason they remain in the past and refuse to move forward?

It is not biblical. The Bible teaches clearly in Romans 10:14-15 that some will "go" and others will "send" them. There is no reason whatsoever to interpret this verse to mean that missionaries must be Western. Yet this is exactly how many North Americans still unconsciously define a missionary.

This attitude is so entrenched that nearly all traditional-style mission boards actually have written, or unwritten, policies prohibiting them from supporting native missionaries!

This prejudice extends into the powerful associations formed by these boards in the United States. I thank God for how He has used these groups to join many mission agencies together in fulfilling the Great Commission. However, both the Evangelical Foreign Missions Association and the Interdenominational Foreign Mission Association by self-definition refuse to allow native mission boards to join their ranks.

Arthur F. Glasser says these mission associations "cannot speak for the whole body of Christ. They represent only the 'sending' half. [This half] cannot shed its national limits nor can it identify with the overseas church. At best it tends thus to be paternalistic, with a tilt towards preserving the status quo."[7]

While it may not be stated as such in their policy manual, the Association of Church Missions Committees also restricts participation by native mission boards. Again, let me say how grateful I am for the positive impact ACMC and other similar organizations are having on churches in the West. Yet the question remains: Are we doing the *most important* thing for the cause of world evangelism? Sadly, the answer is too often no.

I experienced this underlying resistance recently in my conversation with the missions pastor of a large Southern California church. He had invited me to speak at their annual missions conference; I was to be the principal speaker for the whole event. I was encouraged to hear of their $1 million missions budget and thought, "This church must really desire to see the world reached for Christ."

As I talked with the missions pastor, however, I discovered that out of the ten members of their board, nine are retired, colonial-style missionaries. Then I learned that the missions policy of this church specifically states that it will not support indigenous or national missionaries. The only people they support are those sent out from their own church or from related American organizations. I told the missions pastor, "I'll be glad to speak at your church, but you'll have to change your policy."

He smiled sadly and said, "I don't see any hope of that, Brother K.P." Needless to say, I didn't speak at that church.

We are living in an age where over half of the world's population — and the majority of the unreached people — live in countries that restrict Western missionaries. If this church is truly committed to evangelizing the world, sending out their own people should *not* be their number-one priority! Their impact on the world today would be multiplied many times over if they considered indigenous missionaries. But they are stuck in a rut of traditional missions.

This church is a member of ACMC, and it is my understanding that ACMC was initially created for the sake of mobilizing North American churches to become more active in missions. However, restrictive policies such as this one are still common in hundreds of Western churches, despite ACMC's many years of involvement in church programs and in missions.

While a few missions have begun to accept native missionaries as equals, most mission boards and denominations maintain a "North American only" policy.

It is not cost-efficient. According to Gary Schipper, writing in *Evangelical Missions Quarterly*, the average annual cost of maintaining a Western missionary family on the foreign field is now about $43,000.[8] This same amount of money will support an average of forty-three native missionaries in Asia. In most of the Third World mission fields, where the per capita income remains about $300 a year, it is not uncommon for native missionaries to live on $3 to $5 a day.

The twin factors of inflation on the field and increasing costs at home are causing skyrocketing costs in mission support. David J. Hesselgrave cites the example of a friend going to the field today whose support is thirteen times more than his was a generation ago. And his outfit allowance is forty-six times more![9]

Although we have used the figure of $43,000 as the average annual cost of supporting a Western missionary overseas today, we must recognize that this varies from nation to nation and by agency or assignment.

The figures may be especially high for IFMA and EFMA member missions, reported Jack Frizen of the IFMA in an interview. A joint study commissioned by the two mission associations was carried out in early 1990 by Eldon Howard of SIM. His study covered only direct costs to support a missionary, including social security, housing and car allowance, utilities and medical insurance. The average for both associations was only $29,526. These figures do not include home-office administrative and development costs, school fees, travel and costs related to personal ministry.

In direct telephone interviews with several executives of mission boards, all agreed that the $43,000 figure is currently quite typical if one considers *all* the costs — and, in fact, is low for missionaries in Europe and the Far East.

As we do future planning, the cost of supporting Western missionaries becomes increasingly higher. If the average cost of supporting a North American missionary couple were to increase to only $75,000 a year by A.D. 2000 — and if we don't have any increase in the number of missionaries sent — it will cost $5.6 billion just to stay even!

However, a world population projected at six billion in A.D. 2000 requires hundreds of thousands of new missionaries to be sent — perhaps as many as one million gospel workers in order to reach everyone.

Since the United States gave only $1.9 billion to all foreign mission causes, including relief and development aid, in 1989, it is hard to imagine one of the richest nations on earth picking up the tab for the missionary force needed to reach a world population of six billion in A.D. 2000.

Clearly, it is no longer merely inefficient to support only Western missionaries, but it would appear actually cost-prohibitive. North Americans simply cannot afford to operate under the delusion that the world can be won to Christ by sending their own people overseas, particularly if the U.S. dollar continues to devalue at the present rate. Yet this seems to be the basic presupposition of the majority in the North American missions establishment.

Please don't misunderstand me: I am *not* saying the cost involved in sending a missionary should be the highest criterion to determine who goes and who stays. However, we do need to take this factor into strong consideration as we move toward world evangelism.

It is not because Westerners have superior knowledge, faith, love or spirituality. The day of "the white man's burden" is past. There is nothing in Western Christianity or technology that makes it mandatory for the native churches of Asia and Africa to import Western missionary experts.

The primary work of missions — making disciples and establishing churches — is actually often hindered by over-educated, technologically dependent people. Church planting is a work best done by simple servants who are themselves as much as possible like the people they are reaching.

Thus, if Western missionaries are not more effective on the field, why do most traditional-style mission boards still make a North American staff policy the cornerstone of their entire approach to world evangelism? If the following reasons are the motivation, I believe they must be challenged.

(1) *Inertia created by denominational programs, traditions and past movements.* In many churches and groups the foreign missions program is a sentimental bureaucratic tradition that just can't be axed, even though the program staff may long ago have lost the zeal for world evangelism.

Without a fired-up champion to lead the missions program, it can wither and die. Unfortunately, there are always those willing to say, "We've always done it this way."

(2) *A desire to perpetuate pet doctrines and denominations.* This could be true not only of theological teachings, but of church structures and programs as well.

Many missions, in an effort to emphasize a particular school of thought, divide the indigenous church on the mission field along the same doctrinal lines as in the West. They introduce their "distinctives" and biblical interpretations as exclusively correct.

This doesn't apply only to false cults or individuals who have become obsessed with a doctrine. These divisive teachers may be biblically correct but unbalanced in their emphasis. They gain a following by stressing a particular interpretation that would normally be innocent in itself.

However, when any doctrine, even a correct one, is emphasized in a way to develop a personal following and divide the body of Christ, it becomes sinful. And too often so-called correct doctrine is used as a tool to perpetuate or gain power, or create a splinter group.

(3) *A desire to introduce economic or political systems.* This is another variation of dividing the church, but this one is done through politicizing mission agencies and using them to promote particular

economic systems or political schemes of government.

Many conciliar denominations and agencies have fallen into this trap in recent years. They have found that some of their innocuous old mission organizations have been infiltrated by political activists eager to use church agencies to bring about social change secretly.

In a *Reader's Digest* article titled "Do You Know Where Your Church Offerings Go?" Rael Jean Isaac told how one United Methodist group discovered that $442,000 in church funds had gone to fund violent revolutionary movements, including the Palestine Liberation Organization.[10]

Mission agencies make excellent covers in some denominations for individuals whose private agendas would not be accepted by local congregations or even the denomination itself. Some of these have been so radically unbiblical as to include illegal support for armed revolution, political lobbying, and organizing terrorism and violence.

(4) *A hidden desire for power.* Many mission societies continue to exist long after the cause for their formation because the leadership refuses to relinquish control. This was already a problem in the New Testament church. First Peter 5:3 describes such people as "being lords over God's heritage."

These are men and women who, like Diotrephes in 3 John 9, love "to have the preeminence" — lording it over the people of God and exploiting them for personal gain.

Unfortunately, some missions have provided an excellent vehicle for individuals to gain this kind of unholy respect and following, both at home where they raise funds and on the mission field where they lord it over others.

(5) *A desire for adventure, career development and economic gain.* Many youthful staff, I believe, can be attracted to missions for these mixed motivations of the flesh. Some mission recruiters, eager to fill staff gaps on the field, have turned to the use of specialists and short-term workers.

Instead of appealing for simple obedience to the Great Commission, some missions recruitment is turning into a giant job fair with candidates choosing missions based on career development.

These kinds of motives, of course, exist in all of us. However, they are not worthy of the Lord and can be positively dangerous to the mission. Leaders who are driven by such desires can be poor decision-makers.

When called upon to make sober judgments affecting the destiny of lost souls, multitudes of people and even nations, their reasoning can all too often be blinded by self-serving emotions.

This is exactly what can happen in colonial-style missions today. We are faced with multibillion-dollar budgets directed to ineffective programs. We see valuable young lives being wasted by improper assignments. Also, we are faced with twelve thousand *unreached people groups* — billions of people among whom there is no indigenous community of believers large enough or strong enough to evangelize their neighbors.

These billions of lost souls are falling off the edge into an eternity without Christ, while much of the resources of the global church remains preoccupied elsewhere. This is one of the most devastating heritages of traditional-style missions.

It is time to reform those mission agencies that are still flexible and perhaps close down those that have outlived their usefulness. In other words, let's look at the spiritual bottom line and take the action necessary to make missions a profitable spiritual investment.

I believe God continues to call His people from all over the world to reach the lost, and this includes the church in the West as well. It is not an either-or question of the native missionary or the Western missionary. When God calls a man or a woman, he or she must obey.

During the second wave of missionary activity, when William Carey and Hudson Taylor gave their lives to reach the lost, priority number one for the church was to send Western missionaries to go to these heathen lands.

But now times have changed. According to God's plan, in nearly every nation new churches are now being established. Native missionaries are being raised up by God to reach their own people and the neighboring unreached areas. This is the third wave, and I believe the final wave, of missionary movement.

Thus, for the Western church today, priority number one must now be not going, but rather *becoming senders* of this mighty army of native missionaries. Priority number two should be *going as servants* to train and assist our brothers and sisters in finishing this final task.

Notes

[1]W. Dayton Roberts and John A. Siewert, eds., *Mission Handbook: USA/Canada Protestant Ministries Overseas — 14th Edition* (Grand Rapids, Mich.: Zondervan Pub-

lishing House, 1989), p. 5.

[2]David J. Hesselgrave, *Today's Choices for Tomorrow's Mission* (Grand Rapids, Mich.: Zondervan Publishing House, 1988), p. 166.

[3]Samuel Wilson and John Siewert, eds., *Mission Handbook: North American Protestant Missions Overseas — 13th Edition* (Monrovia, Calif.: MARC, 1986), p. 63.

[4]Unpublished study paper by David B. Barrett, *Global Statistics Summary* (Manila, Philippines: Lausanne II Congress on World Evangelization Statistical Task Force, July 11-20, 1989).

[5]David B. Barrett and James W. Reapsome, *Seven Hundred Plans to Evangelize the World* (Birmingham, Ala.: New Hope — AD 2000 Series, 1988), Appendix A, pp. 71-79.

[6]*Ibid.*, pp. 41-42.

[7]Roberts and Siewert, eds., *Mission Handbook — 14th Edition*, p. 42.

[8]Article by Gary Schipper, "Non-Western Missionaries: Our Newest Challenge," *Evangelical Missions Quarterly* (Wheaton, Ill.: Evangelical Missions Information Service, July 1988), p. 199.

[9]Hesselgrave, *Today's Choices for Tomorrow's Mission*, p. 166.

[10]Article reprint by Rael Jean Isaac, "Do You Know Where Your Church Offerings Go?" *Reader's Digest* (Pleasantville, N.Y., 1983), pp. 1-2.

4

White Think

Besides bequeathing to us the current system of sending white missionaries abroad, the colonial era left the mission enterprise of the church with another dubious legacy: a worldwide social services network. This welfare operation has grown so bloated in size and so widespread that the bulk of missions giving in many churches and denominations ultimately ends up here.

In Mark 16:15 Jesus gave us His vision to fulfill: "Go ye into all the world, and preach the gospel to every creature." But it is hard to imagine the church's ever fulfilling that vision until we rethink the priorities of our missions programs. Unless the sending churches of the West work to restore a biblical balance to their missions outreach, the projects and people they support will continue to become increasingly fruitless and ineffective.

To understand the damage this emphasis on social services has done to the overall cause of missions, it is important to note how this relates to the implied social mandate that colonial missionaries carried into their work. This issue is not new to missions. The apostles dealt with it in

Acts 6, and it became a problem again in Victorian colonialism. The hidden social agenda of nineteenth-century missions was very real, even though the missionaries themselves were seldom aware of it.

I am deeply grateful for the commitment and dedication of those early missionaries who left the comforts of their homelands to fulfill the Great Commission. However, like even the most sensitive bicultural missionaries today, they were to some extent prisoners of the time and place in which they were born. They carried with them, to some degree or another, the dominant worldview of the culture that sent them forth: a superiority complex toward the nonindustrialized lands which had been conquered by the West.

Therefore, it is easy to see how the typical colonial-era missionary could be sent to the mission field with a dual motivation: *to convert the heathen to Christianity, thereby helping to bring the benefits of Christian civilization to primitive societies.*

Though seldom actually admitted as such, missionaries envisioned as part of their calling a new world cast in the mold of Christian Europe.

This mentality — the "white man's burden" — had a profound impact on missionary practices and principles then, and it still does today in an updated form. This assumption of cultural and scientific superiority opened a wide door for the present confusion in the very definition of what Christian missions should be all about.

Such a mentality has convinced many Western missionaries today that they have something better to give the natives *in addition to the gospel.* Best-selling author Gayle Erwin (*The Jesus Style*) says it is based on "white think." This is a system of false assumptions that include the following ideas: (1) White people can evangelize the world alone; (2) Third World people are ignorant of the Scripture; (3) Third World people are just plain ignorant; (4) Western technology and prosperity make us better than others; (5) Third World people should submit to us when we go to their countries; (6) we can easily learn the truth by observing and asking questions; (7) Third World churches should adopt Western customs and buildings; (8) Third World people cannot be trusted with money or leadership.[1]

Erwin's list is longer, but these eight points give an idea of what "white think" is all about. In practical terms this kind of approach has opened the door for Western missions to add a great many programs to evangelism — including just about every trade, profession and skill that deals with human services.

Most damaging of all, this "save society" emphasis has scrambled the priorities of sending churches. Most local church leaders and many pastors in the West cannot really state the clear goal of their missions program.

Is social reform, compassionate concern or evangelism to be the driving purpose of missions? Tens of millions of Christians in the United States and Europe cannot reply correctly to this question. Fund-raising promotions have merged the three into one, and the average Christian can no longer separate the gospel of Christ from the various social gospels of religious humanism.

"The future of the world hinges on what we make of this word *mission*," writes Ralph Winter. "Yet at this moment mission is almost universally misunderstood — in both liberal and conservative circles.

"About the only people who still think of mission as having to do with preaching the gospel where Christ is not named — being a testimony to the very last tribe and nation and tongue on this earth — are the oft-confused people in the pew. In this matter their instincts outshine those of many eminent theologians and ecclesiastical statesmen."[2]

And all this confusion has a legitimate basis in history. Social justice and human need were strong motivating forces both for the early missionaries and those who sent them. The list of outstanding social reforms which missionaries brought to the Third World in the last century is a long one. In one colony after another missionaries introduced democracy, elections, education, literacy, modern medicine, printing, sanitation and women's rights.

Amy Carmichael, who gave fifty-five years of service to India without a furlough, helped change the direction of a nation. The fellowship she organized in Dohnavur helped save thousands of children from the degradation of temple prostitution.

In addition, her unrelenting revelations of the secret temple rituals finally pressured Hindu and government leaders to ban the despicable practice of "marrying children to the gods" — a custom that made adolescent girls available sexually to male worshippers of Hindu idols.[3]

But not all such attempts to bring the fruits of Christian civilization to native populations were as successful, especially when the tree of Christian faith had not yet had time to take root itself. The sordid history of pressured conversions and mass baptisms and the premature institution of civil religion in many parts of Latin America created some of the most regrettable chapters in the story of colonial-era missions.

Some missionary efforts to influence culture have an almost comic character in retrospect. Missionary attempts to add brassieres and neckties to the native wardrobe and build gothic chapels in the tropics probably deserved the rich ridicule and humor that has since grown up around them.

No one involved in missions today of whatever theological persuasion can escape association with the history of traditional missions, in both its positive and negative sides.

In retrospect, however, many of the vast efforts at social engineering by missionaries were kind, gentle and helpful, even if they were not always biblical or effective. No one can deny that some of the most progressive changes in colonial society were wrought through the creation of thousands of nineteenth-century institutions. Mission hospitals, leprosariums, orphanages and schools became the most visible evidence of missionary presence during the Great Century from the mid-1800s to 1939.

The Rise of Missionary Institutions

These institutions had a sweetness about them that seemed to charm everyone, including the missionaries themselves. Many argued that switching to the institutional approach would create a positive identity for missionaries in the community, opening "unlimited opportunities" for evangelism and witness.

Also, it was argued that as people were healed and educated by Christians, they would automatically develop an interest in Jesus, the gospel and the church. Although history has proven these theories often to be fantasy, there is no mistaking the positive public relations value these missionary institutions had at the time.

Furthermore, institutional work created goodwill toward the church and missions from indigenous populations, the secular and religious media, and supporters in the homeland.

In difficult political times these humanitarian institutions gave missionaries a legitimate and useful reason to remain in the colonies. Their economic impact was great. They created many jobs for nationals, both in the institution itself and in the surrounding community. Whole towns and neighborhoods grew up around some mission hospitals and schools.

The institutions themselves often became important sources of financial income for the mission and national church — from outright donations as well as from fees and tuitions.

No wonder, then, that by the turn of the century missionary clinics and schools were well-established almost everywhere, usually following the railways and waterways into the farthest interiors of every continent.

Denominational mission boards in the sending nations and their furloughing missionaries appealed for funds to pioneer and operate these institutions, thus effectively blurring the lines between evangelistic and humanitarian programs in the minds of home-church supporters.

Except for a few brave exceptions, such as Anglican missionary to China Roland Allen and Henry Venn of the Church Missionary Society, nineteenth-century church leaders treated the institutional approach as normative.

Allen, who would later write several mission classics including *Missionary Methods: St. Paul's or Ours?*, was one of the lone voices who wrote and spoke out against the rising tide of evangelism by institution.

Charles Henry Long and Anne Rowthorn, writing of Allen, say he "questioned the priority given to schools and similar institutional work over evangelism. By establishing schools and hospitals and committing to them, rather than to the churches, the bulk of their budgets and personnel, missionary societies were not only trying to take 'the best of the West' to backward peoples but to establish new cultural norms for them. In its extreme form this strategy led to the assumption that Western higher education was not only an expression of, but almost a precondition for, the life of the church."[4]

Henry Venn wrote of the "euthanasia" of missions as early as 1854 and began using the *"three self"* terms to describe the coming indigenous church for the first time. He argued not for institutions, but mission agencies that would create self-governing, self-supporting and self-propagating churches and then "die out."[5]

The movement toward a social gospel was so broad in English and American Protestantism that it is difficult to put a finger on one man, one date or one movement that was pivotal. However, if one name stands out above all others, it would have to be William Booth.

Booth's life and ministry have challenged me to the core, and I thank

God for raising up this man to reach his generation. A Methodist missionary to the slums of London, Booth dramatically combined humanitarianism and evangelism into what eventually became known as the Salvation Army. As one of the most famous of many new missions formed during this period, the Salvation Army concentrated solely on what would now be described as a "wholistic ministry" and spread around the world in less than twenty-five years. Virtually every colony had a lively Salvation Army presence, and many other organizations duplicated its programming style and techniques.

Many committed evangelical leaders loaned their names and support to help found such organizations as the YMCA, and these humanitarian spinoffs of the church spread to every corner of the globe.

Not surprisingly, the majority of missions and their supporting churches jumped on the social-service bandwagon to some extent.

However, the primary focus of these social organizations has begun to drift away from evangelism. Few stopped to compare these popular theologies with the teachings of Jesus and the apostles about the Great Commission. Social reform, charity and evangelism were equated in the minds of millions. And so by the turn of the century social services had become an unchallenged part of the warp and woof of missions. To many, in fact, social services *were* missions, and this was a misconception that some missionaries felt quite comfortable in perpetuating. It took the offense of the cross away and gave them an easily accepted platform on which to stand.

The Tragic Harvest of the Social Gospel

Two world wars and a Great Depression later, the liberal belief in the ultimate goodness of mankind — and the hope of "heaven on earth" — had been rocked to its very foundations. The philosophical and theological underpinnings of the social gospel were gone.

Institutional evangelism had already proven itself ineffective in making converts or establishing Christian churches. It wasn't until the decades following independence that missionary advocates of education, health and welfare were to see the tragic results of their misguided zeal.

The hoped-for Christian presence in post-colonial governments seldom materialized. When it did, it was soon snuffed out by anti-Christian forces.

Far from ushering in the kingdom of God, in many cases the schools and universities founded by missionaries were themselves taken over and used as bases for terrorism and bloodshed!

In what is now Myanmar, the American Baptist University of Rangoon was nationalized along with all other mission schools and hospitals in 1960. After the missionaries were deported and Burmese church leaders were removed, the school was used to propagate a Marxist projection for Myanmar's future. As I write this book, the University of Rangoon continues to turn out the ruling elite for one of the most corrupt and oppressive governments in the world.

In China the Presbyterian Seminary in Nanjing became the headquarters of the Great Cultural Revolution, which persecuted millions of Christians and led to many senseless deaths. Today it is the center of the Communist party-controlled Three Self Patriotic Church. It is still associated with the oppression of Christians and religious freedom in the People's Republic. The YMCA in Shanghai, once the flagship of a vast network of Chinese Y's, was actually turned into a center of torture and murder by the Red Guards during the Great Cultural Revolution.

In India, as hundreds of Christian schools and hospitals have come under government control, they are often used now to propagate secular humanism more effectively than they propagated Christianity under missionary control.

Furthermore, there are frequent stories in the Indian media of converts from these missions who have now reverted to animism, Hinduism and idolatry! Christian hospitals and the mission compounds around them often attracted so-called rice Christians — converts who joined the church primarily for material gain. When the mission payroll ended, so did their faith.

In Tanzania, where all missionaries were driven out following liberation, the government is only now allowing a handful of Western missionaries back — on the condition that they serve in secularized development programs. Often the only benefits apparent from years of social work are invitations to do more social work.

In Africa, where Christian missions are now heavily involved in providing relief, development and nation-building services, their ministries are opening few new doors for evangelistic witness.

Even in countries that have remained open to the West, continued institutional outreach has had little impact on evangelism. Two clear

Asian examples are Nepal and Thailand.

In both countries, where there are extensive networks of Christian institutions involving hundreds of foreign missionaries, too few Christian converts can be traced to the work of institutions.

In Thailand it is true that churches have been started in Chaing Mai, Monoram and Bangkok near Christian hospitals. A close examination of the work, however, reveals that most of these churches would have formed anyway, regardless of the institutions associated with them.

These are not selected examples. The story is almost the same wherever one looks. Institutions are ineffective methods to win converts or plant churches. Few missionaries working in an institutional context, by the very nature of the structural constraints, can do effective evangelism. Furthermore, by their calling and gifts, they are often unsuited for discipleship and church-planting outreach, the essential elements of any Great Commission ministry.

Notes

[1]Article by Gayle Erwin, "How to Overcome 'White Think' in Cross Cultural Ministries," *Servant Quarters* (Cathedral City, Calif.: Summer 1989), pp. 1-7.

[2]Article by Ralph Winter, "The Meaning of 'Mission'," *Mission Frontiers* (Pasadena, Calif.: U.S. Center for World Mission, July 1987), p. 3.

[3]Ruth A. Tucker, *From Jerusalem to Irian Jaya* (Grand Rapids, Mich.: Zondervan Publishing House, 1983), pp. 240-241.

[4]Article, "The Legacy of Roland Allen," by Charles Henry Long and Anne Rowthorn, *International Bulletin of Missionary Research* (New Haven, Conn.: Overseas Ministries Study Center, April 1989), p. 65.

[5]Stephen Neill, *A History of Christian Missions* (Baltimore, Md.: Pelican Books, 1964), pp. 259-260.

Who Goes Where and
Does What?

Missions, including even the most evangelical ones, seem not to
have learned their lessons from the past failure of social work.
Many mission executives, frustrated by government restrictions on evangelistic work, still cling to the concept of institutions and
social work because it is often the only way they can get a visa to stay in
the country.

It is amazing how many evangelical missionaries still claim they
engage in social work because they believe it will provide opportunities
to witness. This despite the fact that year after year they continue to show
little evangelistic results for their efforts and expense.

According to the admittedly outdated studies of personnel distribution
in overseas missions collected in 1987 by MARC, only 33 percent of all
Western missionaries said they were primarily involved in attempting to
communicate the gospel to non-Christians. Another 29 percent said they
were attempting to support existing churches, and 38 percent said they
were involved in "other ministries."[1]

Other statistics appear to indicate that less than 33 percent are truly involved in frontline evangelism.

At the time this chapter was written, InterCristo, the leading evangelical placement organization, listed just over 5,000 overseas openings for missionary positions. Only 86 of the openings were for pioneer evangelism and church planting among unreached people. Another 492 were for church positions that included church planting as well as chaplaincies, urban evangelism, child evangelism, discipleship and worship.

But 4,422 of the 5,000 positions were for other specialties, mostly social services! More than 89 percent of the current job openings in missions were for nonevangelism, nondiscipleship job descriptions!

What are mission agencies looking for today? Here are some of the more unusual samples on the InterCristo opportunity list: a solar engineer in Zaire, a fiberglass molder in Pakistan, a craft supervisor in Nepal, a forester in Kenya and a carpet layer in Japan!

During a radio interview in 1988 a knowledgeable missionary from one of the largest evangelical denominations in the United States said he believed fewer than one thousand of their three thousand-plus missionaries were involved in any kind of work that "used the Bible." Not one missionary family was reported to be doing pioneer church-planting work among an unreached people group. This particular mission agency has an annual budget of over $50 million.

A glance through a random sampling of the help-wanted lists of leading IFMA and EFMA mission boards shows that only a small percentage of the open positions on the field today are for church planting or evangelistic missionaries.

Instead, the need list includes an amazing variety of occupations: administrators, secretaries, health-care providers, construction workers, linguists, mechanics, computer programmers, electricians, music, English, math and science teachers, and transportation workers.

These are the kinds of workers the *most strongly evangelical* mission boards are seeking. Even fewer missionary positions are offered for soul-winners in the older, less-evangelical churches and denominations.

For example, Bishop C. Dale White, an important ecumenical leader in New York, recently attacked the Mission Society for United Methodists, saying that its practice of sending evangelists overseas is "completely out of touch with reality." In an article in the *Dallas Times Herald* he is quoted as saying that the evangelical Methodist group was a "divisive force" for suggesting a return to spiritual ministries.[2]

I have found that Bishop White's view is shared by most of the thirty-member denominations of the National Council of Churches — and regrettably by some conservative evangelical church leaders as well.

Yet the majority of American churches continue to send some missionary staff overseas — usually with denominations or missions historically associated with their founders. Invariably, many of these workers find themselves involved in maintenance activities of programs such as Christian education, theological education and social work.

Evangelistic missionaries are so rare in older denominations that they are all but nonexistent. For example, a qualified spokesperson for the Protestant Episcopal Church in the U.S.A., who was interviewed for this book, said that *less than one-tenth of 1 percent* of their three hundred appointed overseas missionaries are primarily involved in evangelism and church planting.

Denominational leadership, both conservative evangelical and liberal, often establishes relationships with sister-churches on mission fields. Because of this there is a strong tendency to assume Third World evangelism is complete — or is the sole responsibility of the indigenous church.

This leaves the door open for North American missionaries to put their emphasis on helping to maintain existing churches and providing social services as "a witness" to secular society.

The National Council of Churches therefore focuses most of the remaining missionary zeal left in the historic, mainline churches through its Church World Service division. In an interview for this book, a representative of CWS reported that its $39.6 million budget last year went for an array of social-economic programs such as:
- $1.5 million to dig wells and distribute water in India;
- $170,000 to provide schooling and health care to street children in Brazil and Peru;
- $2 million for famine relief in the southern Sudan.

Development is the current buzzword used by the missionary social workers involved with conciliar associations. Rural development includes many programs so secularized that entire staffs are not even nominally Christian, such as the Muslim workers hired to run so-called Christian credit unions for Indonesian villages.

According to one spokesman interviewed for this chapter, at the Division of Overseas Ministries (DOM-NCCUSA) the personnel are not directly involved in proselytism but "leave the work of evangelism to member churches overseas."

Many of these highly politicized programs go far beyond the simple charitable and relief efforts which are the thrust of emotional fund-raising appeals, and so by design they are almost always separated from the proclamation of the gospel.

Liberation Theology, Politics and Terrorism

As liberation theology has captured the imagination and support of church leaders and missionaries, a greater amount of funds and other support from Western churches have found their way into the hands of Marxist revolutionaries. In addition, a small but growing number of missionaries have become politically and often violently activated.

Fidel Castro in 1984 said, "Liberation theology is doing more to promote revolutionary change in Latin America than all the millions of books on Marxism had been able to achieve."[3]

By sharing in grants to combat racism, promote human rights and provide humanitarian assistance, thousands of churches and Christian ministries in the West are providing assistance to left-wing political causes on every continent. Often this funding contributes to the deaths of countless innocent people as a result of revolutionary violence.

That some missionaries should embrace a violent form of social change as a shortcut to the kingdom of God is not really surprising to the serious student of mission history. If social justice becomes the prime motivator for missions, then the errors of liberation theology follow naturally. Carl F.H. Henry, in passing judgment on the liberation movement, says, "It is tragic that in its call to social justice Liberation Theology should so sadly have missed the biblical way."[4]

Daily revelations of new political involvement in the name of Christ are a sobering reminder of how dangerous it is to stray away from the Great Commission mandate in any mission activity.

What About Missionary Tentmakers?

In addition to direct missionary social work, there is a popular movement today urging Western Christians to go overseas as bivocational "missionary tentmakers," again mostly as advisers, educators, social workers and technicians.

More than one thousand such tentmakers are teaching English in China at this time according to one well-informed source. Tentmakers who were interviewed in China repeatedly said the Chinese government prefers Christians for these positions.

Unlike missionary social work, which directly drains support funds away from evangelism and church-planting work, most of these tentmakers are supposedly earning a regular salary overseas and therefore should not have to raise support in the sending churches. These tentmakers should be witnessing in their daily lives as every Christian is called to, and in that work they certainly deserve the prayers and encouragement of missions-minded congregations.

However, the following flags of caution must be raised whenever this kind of outreach is loosely labeled as "missionary":

How free will the tentmaker be to witness? Many Muslim and other closed countries insist that such workers sign nonprosclytizing agreements forbidding witnessing for Christ. How can a tentmaker sign such an agreement with a clear conscience?

How much free time will the tentmaker have off the job to spend in discipling converts and forming churches? Often tentmaking work for foreigners involves high-level job responsibilities that overlap into free time, preventing the tentmaker from having enough unscheduled time to do true missionary work. Any successful bivocational ministry overseas requires that the tentmaker have long periods of free time. A secular job would distract from one-on-one disciple-making, small-group meetings and the other extended periods needed for witnessing and follow-up.

How much freedom will the tentmaker have to move openly in local society? Unless the tentmaker lives in a dormitory or other intimate situation such as a private home, crossing cultural and language barriers may still be extremely frustrating.

Many tentmaking positions require the expatriate to work in isolated and difficult circumstances quite separate from the people of the land.

Often tentmaking positions in management require the foreigner to be involved in local politics and avoid involvement in religion and the lives of the common people.

Some English teacher tentmakers in China have had extraordinary opportunities to witness for Christ and have even started small Bible-study groups on campus. There is no doubt that many tentmakers grow spiritually during their time there. But cross-cultural missionary work must not be viewed as a time to "discover one's own ministry" or experiment with personal callings on Third World populations!

Gayle Erwin has said it so well: "If you have not developed your capabilities and proven your ministry here at home, do not expect that you can do so over there. To be a tourist and observe might be appropriate, but to go to another country to 'find' your ministry is to become an instant burden to them. First of all, your thoughts are inward as you still develop and find yourself, and you are unable to be truly others-centered.

"Second, you absorb their energies as they try to figure out just what to do with you without hurting you. Just because you are white does not mean that other countries welcome you with open arms. Most countries will not give you a long-term visa unless you have skills that are needed and in short supply. The kingdom is not in short supply of people trying to 'find' themselves."[5]

In summary, *can you tentmake and still preach the Word?* We need to remember that in these tentmaking or "social work" situations, nothing ever happens for God until somebody presents the gospel. The missionary must have freedom and time to present the Word of God clearly and openly. Disciples must be made and then formed into living churches. This alone is valid, New Testament missionary work, the only kind that should be considered for financial support from sending churches.

The term *tentmaking* comes from the apostle Paul's practice of supporting himself in the tentmaking industry while preaching the gospel. But his primary activity was evangelistic, not the making of tents.

However, tentmaking holds exciting promises, and it will be interesting to see how this kind of outreach develops over the coming years.

Notes

[1]Samuel Wilson and John Siewert, eds., *Mission Handbook: North American Protestant Missions Overseas — 13th Edition* (Monrovia, Calif.: MARC, 1986), p. 616.

[2]Article, unsigned, "Methodist Bishop Blasts Group's Overseas Mission," *Dallas Morning News*, July 8, 1988.

[3]Quoted in article by David W. Balsiger, "Liberation Theology Special Edition," *Family Protection Scoreboard* (Costa Mesa, Calif.: National Citizens Action Network, 1989), p. 51.

[4]*Ibid.*, p. 25.

[5]Article by Gayle Erwin, "How to Overcome 'White Think' in Cross Cultural Ministries," *Servant Quarters* (Cathedral City, Calif.: Summer 1989), p. 2.

— 6 —

What About Social Justice and Compassion?

Doesn't the Bible, particularly the Old Testament, have a strong emphasis on compassion, social justice and charity? you may ask.

No one could deny that. Socio-political involvement is clearly expected by a just and righteous God. Old Testament law makes provision for the aliens, the poor and the widowed. Through the Law of Moses God demanded that all oppressed and exploited people be protected.

The laws of Jubilee, gleaning, the Sabbath and tithes show God's concern and provision for the poor in society. Some of the most terrible Old Testament judgments fell upon Israel, Sodom and Gomorrah for their exploitation of the poor and needy.

A comparison of Old and New Testaments shows that there can be no argument about the Christian's clear social responsibility. (See Gen. 1:26-27, 18:25; Lev. 19:18; Ps. 45:7; Is. 1:17; Matt. 5:20, 6:33; Luke 6:27,35; James 2:14-26, 3:9.) However, evangelism is not social action. The Great Commission is not a mandate for political liberation. Disciple-making is not charity, although at times it may involve charity.

So while we as individuals and local churches must speak out and be involved in the work of reconciliation and compassion, that doesn't mean we should call it missions. Nor can God's laws for justice and mercy in the nation of Israel be considered a mission mandate for the church to seek social justice as a ministry category.

The cutting edge of biblical, New Testament missions is proclamation, conversion and disciple-making that leads to the establishment of local churches. Any time this basic task is confused with political or social action, missions lose the essence of their integrity and power.

The New Testament apostles turned the world upside down not by digging wells or building hospitals, but by proclaiming the Word of God, which is sharper than any two-edged sword.

Social Work in the New Testament

But isn't social work a valid New Testament ministry? Didn't Jesus and the apostles concern themselves with the needs of the whole man? Isn't social work even without soul-winning and church planting a legitimate ministry in its own right? Why shouldn't missionary social workers be sent overseas because there is a needy world out there?

The only way to answer these questions is to survey quickly the popular New Testament texts that have been used to advocate social work. They need to be studied in context. We need to see if these proof-texts can truly be applied or equated to the work of the Great Commission.

Didn't Jesus feed the hungry and heal the sick — and aren't we supposed to do the works that He did? (See Matt. 14:21, 20:34; Mark 7:37; Luke 8:54-55; John 9:7, 14:12.)

Those who ask this question may agree with J. Philip Hogan, executive director of the division of foreign missions for the Assemblies of God. He says, "Many people feel that the church should engage in social assistance only for the purpose of prying open doors for the gospel in restricted access countries. But if that is our motive for providing assistance to hurting people, then we are the ones who need the help....I want the world to know that the reason we do these things is because Jesus Christ did them.

"If our providing social assistance opens doors that would otherwise be closed to the missionary endeavors...good! But if not, we will still continue to provide relief. Because opening doors is not our reason for sharing in other people's sufferings. Demonstrating the truth of Christ's words and sharing the love of God are our intent."[1]

There is no quarrel with the way Jesus again and again demonstrated His love and compassion in miracles of healing and provision, but that was only incidental to His main purpose.

Our Lord's miracles of feeding and healing were basically signs to prove His identity as Messiah, as He told the disciples of John in Matthew 11:2-5 and Luke 7:18-22. Jesus miraculously and symbolically showed compassion to the sick and needy, but His mission here was obviously not to end hunger and disease. If He had wanted to do so, He could have ended all hunger, injustice and disease at any time with a single word.

In Luke 19:10 Jesus stated His primary mission clearly: "For the Son of man is come to seek and to save that which was lost." Jesus knew that the main problem of mankind is sin, and that's why His primary mission was to die on the cross to deliver us from it.

The Great Commission, repeated five times in the Gospels and Acts, stresses preaching and teaching as the main activities of the first missionaries. Obviously, social action and compassionate ministries were not critical to this work or Jesus would have included them in the marching orders He gave His apostles.

Didn't the early church sell all they had to provide for the needy? (See Acts 4:32-37.)

Yes, it is obvious that the New Testament church, at least in Jerusalem, had an extensive program of social services for widows and orphans within their own membership (see Acts 6:1-3 and 1 Tim. 5:1-16). But the emphasis in these passages is never on meeting the needs of the world or on using social welfare programs as an evangelistic technique.

In fact, when Peter and the other apostles were asked to get involved in the social work in Acts 6:4, they actually declined! "But we will give ourselves continually to prayer, and to the ministry of the word," said the twelve. Prayer and preaching were their missionary priorities, although it is clear they made provision here for this important ministry of the local church.

The apostles, our first missionary examples in the Bible, appointed deacons from the local body to oversee social work. How ironic it is that we today have switched this around so that we are, in effect, sending our "deacons" abroad to provide social services for people who are not even Christians, let alone members of our local churches.

Didn't Paul collect emergency relief funds for the saints in Jerusalem on his third missionary journey? (See Rom. 15:25-26.)

Yes, but once again here is an exception rather than the rule. This is the only time he collects relief funds — in an emergency — and he does it to help others in the body of Christ. In 2 Corinthians 8-9 we see that these funds were collected for the brethren and not done for outreach purposes to the world as is so common today.

Does this imply that emergency relief and assistance to unbelievers are wrong? Of course not, but we also cannot say that disaster aid and famine relief are required as part of the Great Commission. Nor dare we somehow imagine that rice shipments or milk supplements are evangelism — or even an effective witness for Christ of any kind.

To argue that such aid is a viable Christian witness, some form of evangelism or even biblical Christian missions is at best fuzzy theology. Its worst case comes when such social aid is presented as a reasonable substitute for evangelism in our church mission budgets.

There will always be disasters, famines and wars that call upon us to send what relief we can, and Christians will continue to do so as we have since the beginning. But it is imperative that we keep such activity in proper perspective. A recent editorial in *Mountain Movers* says it well:

"Ministries of compassion are temporal remedies at best. The church is not here to make this present world better, because this present world is condemned. And Jesus never commissioned His church to clean up this world. He commissioned His church to snatch men's hearts out of this world and set them on a path to another world — an eternal, spiritual world.

"So we tenaciously follow the pattern of the early church. They cared for suffering humanity. But they were careful to make certain that those ministries did not replace their primary reason for being — the preaching of the gospel.

"Unless their corporate activities ultimately led to the winning of souls and the planting of indigenous churches, they altered those activities. And any activity that supersedes that objective today must also be expunged from the church's agenda."[2]

Didn't Jesus say that when you help the poor, it is the same as helping Him? (See Matt. 25:40.)

This verse is frequently taken out of context, especially for missionary offerings and appeal letters. Jesus said that when you assist "the least of

70

these my brethren, you have done it unto me." Who are His brethren? Jesus made it clear in Mark 3:35 that His brethren are those who do the will of God — not everyone in the world, as is frequently heard in the mission appeals for relief. Therefore, social work cannot be justified as an evangelistic technique or require us to operate billion-dollar relief and development programs in the name of Christ. Of course, every Christian is required to show compassion for other believers who are hungry, in need or imprisoned.

What about Jesus' parable of the good Samaritan? Doesn't that teach us to help our neighbors? (See Luke 10:30-37.)

There are many lessons in this parable, but the main point is a warning against religious legalism and hypocrisy. Any God-fearing believer is an incredible hypocrite if he or she obeys the letter of the law but breaks the spirit of it by ignoring a needy person. The Pharisee and lawyer here put religious ceremony and ritual ahead of love, perverting the whole Law of Moses. That was the main lesson Jesus was trying to make in this passage.

Emergency care for strangers and the homeless, as well as relief for the widows and orphans among us, is obviously a legitimate *personal ministry of every Christian. But the New Testament teaches that this is to be practiced primarily as individuals or through the local church as outlined in 1 Timothy 5:1-16. The early believers would have understood this because synagogue and temple tithes were used to help the needy.*

Again, these verses and others do not establish missionary development and relief ministries as such. Yet today billions of dollars are involved in this so-called missions work. Charity has been turned into a business that often dwarfs the ministry of true missions.

Whenever this happens, those in leadership must bring back the correct balance. Proclamation and teaching must be restored to their primary place. Then, as the gospel changes lives, individual Christians will play their normal role of "salt and light" in society. This method in the long run brings far more beneficial social change to a community than short-term programs that seek to force radical change on already-established structures.

Give Us Back Our Basic Mandate!

As billions of dollars continue to be siphoned off into secondary missions programs, it is time that remedial action be taken to restore the biblical balance to current missions programs.

The challenge facing leaders of any reformation in missions now is to separate frontline evangelistic mission efforts from social work. As long as there are over two *billion* lost souls who have never heard the gospel — and twelve thousand unreached people groups without a witness — the need for New Testament missionaries is overwhelming.

Plainly, the focus of missions must concentrate on placing qualified evangelists and church planters among hidden people groups and in unreached areas of the harvest field that have been neglected for too many centuries.

Modern mission agencies have hopelessly confused this still-incomplete pioneer work with maintenance programs for existing churches, with support services and with humanitarian-aid programs.

A gross error, of course, would be to deny the validity of these other ministries. They have a place, but it must be a subordinate one to the central work of presenting the gospel.

However, the crisis in Western missions today is not that the church is neglecting temporal and physical needs — quite the contrary. Any analysis of the trends in our missions budgets will show that we are majoring on the minors. Modern missions has been seriously sidetracked by sincere but misguided idealists, and it is important for those who understand the necessary balance to restore biblical priorities.

If church and mission leaders in the West don't act soon, those in the pews must. Recently, a women's group in a mainline denominational church spoke out — through their checkbooks — when they discovered where their missions dollars were going.

The women notified their denomination's women's division that they were withholding half of their yearly pledge. Their reason: concern over the leftist orientation of some of the recipients of their money.

One such recipient turned out to be involved in radical leftist politics, which included a plan to remove members of the U.S. administration who were opposed to Marxist activity in Central America.

These ladies found out that their denomination has given tens of thousands of dollars over the last three years to this organization, which still continues to raise thousands of dollars every month to support its activities.

The conclusion is simple but not easy. Every believer must personally re-examine every cause and mission that gets his or her support.

Learning how to make valid judgment calls and establishing systems that will send support to the missionaries who are really doing pioneer work — these are the challenges of the 1990s and beyond.

Satan has presented us with an alluring array of substitutes for the Great Commission. We need to wait humbly upon God for discernment about the validity of the mission causes that get His tithes and offerings.

Notes

[1]Article by J. Philip Hogan, "Because Jesus Did," *Mountain Movers* (Springfield, Mo.: Assemblies of God, Division of Foreign Missions, June 1989), pp. 10-11.

[2]*Ibid.*

Who Is a
True Missionary?

I was trying as best I could to comfort a dear Christian leader in our Carrollton, Texas, office. He sat across from me in shock and despair, completely devastated by rejection.

As an Indian citizen, he had recently earned his doctorate in theology at a leading seminary. A brilliant Christian teacher, he is one of those rare geniuses whom God has gifted with a command of four languages, capable of reading, writing and preaching in each one.

His family was converted to Christ through the ministry of a leading colonial-era denominational mission, in India for generations. Mission officials had encouraged him to leave his wife and children in India and come to the United States for further education. In fact, leaders of his denomination pointed to his achievements as a "trophy of grace" — one of the triumphs of their long missionary labors in South Asia.

So it was only natural that my Indian brother would want to return to his homeland as a missionary to his own people and that he would apply to that same denominational mission board for support. Since Americans from the society can no longer receive missionary visas for India, he assumed the mission would want to send him back to carry on and extend the work. He was in for a rude awakening.

His application was graciously received by the American board. They wrote back an effusive letter of praise, affirming the brother and expressing sympathy and moral support for his calling. However, they "regretted" that they had to refuse his application because it "conflicted with their bylaws" to send out a native missionary — no matter how qualified.

Although their bylaws didn't say it in so many words, they confirmed in writing the popular definition of a missionary. That is, the person must possess North American citizenship.

What Should Determine Missionary Qualifications?

Who truly is a missionary? It would be easy to answer the question if most Christian leaders still used the New Testament to form their definition. The Bible clearly gives the basic qualifications for missionary service.

Unfortunately, in the real world of missions today New Testament standards for Christian service play such an insignificant role in missionary selection that the Lord Jesus Himself — and probably most of the apostles — would not even get through the screening process for their first interview. Ironically, well-connected, educated, middle-class, affluent and politically oriented Judas might have "the right stuff" to score well on his application.

Since the screening procedures for missionary service today remain rooted in the colonial-era concept of missions, it should come as no surprise to see that the qualifying process is still prisoner to some of the most prejudiced cultural norms of the nineteenth century.

To be perfectly honest, many mission societies make their staffing decisions much as did the Pharisees in Jesus' day. They have added a *Talmud* of their own to the *Torah* — a book of commentary and interpretations of Scripture. Decisions are made, therefore, not based on the Bible, but on the traditions and interpretations of men. How the Lord Jesus despised and denounced this practice!

Yet these modern-day Pharisees have added a code of standards and rules to Scripture that are formed primarily by Western culture. They appear as blind to their sin as the New Testament Pharisees were in the days when Jesus walked this earth.

Here are at least six major examples of unbiblical standards.

Educational degrees. Most missions require a Western liberal arts education for all new candidates, or at least a college degree and some minimum amount of Bible school training. Many mission boards now give preference to those with master's degrees or other advanced degrees.[1]

What this has to do with successful pioneer missions work is beyond comprehension. In reality a Western university education or even theological training is often more a hindrance than a help on the mission field. In frontline situations it can erect another barrier that has to be overcome in relating to lost souls.

Indeed, most native Christians find that a Western education has to be consciously unlearned before they can begin to minister to their own people!

How different this emphasis on formal education is from Jesus and the disciples. Jesus was obviously a home-schooled rabbi who didn't train in the leading seminaries of Jerusalem. Instead, He had worked with His hands as a common carpenter. Like most of the disciples, who were also "blue-collar workers," He lacked a formal education.

The Pharisees, in fact, criticized the first missionaries as "unlearned and ignorant men" (Acts 4:13). I don't believe for a minute they were actually ignorant or unlearned, since they had studied three years with Jesus, the Son of God. But by the standards of men they appeared to be.

My point is not that ignorant missionaries are desirable. We must never stop learning. Missionaries need as much practical Bible training and experience in the ministry as possible. However, we must also understand that very little of this kind of training ever comes from the formal, Western education still being required by colonial-style mission societies.

Health and psychological testing. I once heard a mission executive state that his organization was not a hospital but a fighting army. Wounded soldiers, learners and people with problems need not apply! When problems surfaced in the life of a missionary, this brother eliminated that person from his organization as fast and as quietly as possible.

This unnatural emphasis on health and perfection in Western missions also extends to a distinct prejudice against recruiting older people. It is interesting that Jesus began His ministry at a rather mature thirty, an age that would be the limit for many mission societies today.

Class and background checks. Through letters of reference, interviews and phone calls, Western mission boards select staff who are most socially compatible with themselves. Unbiblical standards such as denominational distinctives, race, ethnic heritage, age and social class become important determining factors.

Jesus was a king who gave up His kingdom to be born a human baby and live a life of simplicity in an obscure village. He identified with the lowest classes of His society and was not afraid to be seen associating with prostitutes and corrupt politicians. The church leaders of His day hated Jesus for this so much that they plotted to kill Him.

Talents and skills. "This is the day of the missionary specialist," proclaims recruiting literature for missionaries at mission conventions for Christian students.

The fastest-growing emphasis in Western missions today is on secular technologies and training such as aviation, anthropology, broadcasting, computerization, construction, electronics, engineering, linguistics, marketing, media, medicine, nursing, rural and village development, sociology, social work and teaching.

This accent in modern Western missions continues the shift to physical and mental abilities rather than concerns of the Holy Spirit and the inner man. This began in the last century, as pioneer missionary institutions required the first educational and medical specialists.

Of course, there is a legitimate need for some skilled personnel. I am not against them, but the emphasis has gone so far the other way that reliance on the supernatural appears to play only a minor role in Western-based missions. The technocrats seem to be calling the shots, not spiritual leaders.

Expatriation. Some missiologists have gone so far as to include this as part of the very definition of a missionary. They claim that unless a person actually leaves his or her homeland, he or she is not qualified to be called a missionary! Others vary this theme, insisting that one is not a missionary unless he or she is doing cross-cultural ministry.

Roberta Winter and Richard Cotten address this issue in the July 1990 issue of the *Global Prayer Digest*: "What is a missionary? A missionary is someone who is sent to witness of his faith cross-culturally. Can he be a native? Not technically speaking. If he is a 'native' of the culture where he works, then he is not witnessing cross-culturally. Therefore the term 'native missionary' is self-contradictory."[2]

I am saddened by this continued insistence to split hairs on terminology. Why is the focus on where native missionaries can and cannot go, instead of helping them to reach the unreached wherever they are?

What about the Lord's constant emphasis on taking the gospel to the Jews first? This was missionary work within His own culture, and it was where the Father instructed Him to place the accent in His outreach. For Jesus, cross-cultural witness was the exception not the rule.

In fact, nowhere in the Scriptures were the apostles required to cross cultures to qualify for missionary service. Apparently, a few of the early apostles served most of their missionary lives in Jerusalem and Judea. Throughout history some of the most successful missionaries have been men like St. Patrick — a missionary who went back to his own people in Ireland after his conversion.

Given the reality of the mission field today, it would be foolish for us to require all missionaries to leave their home cultures. The best current examples are in China, India and the U.S.S.R. There, millions still have not received the gospel in villages that are within the cultural reach of existing congregations. Native missionaries can be sent to them without crossing cultural barriers. They also can go to close-by cultures where the barriers are relatively weak compared to what they would be for Western missionaries.

Few of the unreached people groups in our modern world are reachable by cross-cultural missionaries from the West. Even though reaching them requires some cross-cultural work, *this is best done by those from nearby cultures.*

As this book was going to press I heard a shocking story. Perhaps the most troubling thing of all was that not much has changed in missions today, despite efforts to change the status quo.

After graduating from a foremost Christian liberal arts college, Vicky (not her real name) sensed God's call on her life for missions. She left soon afterward for the Philippines under the auspices of a leading denominational mission agency.

While she was there she met a Filipino believer I'll call Matt, who was involved in mission work in his country. It was only a matter of time before they knew the Lord was joining their lives together.

Matt and Vicky traveled to the States for their wedding and now plan to return to the Philippines as soon as they raise their support.

However, they will not be returning under the same agency that sent

Vicky. In a letter she wrote to one of our staff, she explained the startling reason. When they approached their mission board with a request to send them both to the Philippines, the headquarters responded: "[The mission has] a policy," says Vicky, "that they do not send nationals as missionaries to their home countries...[Matt] is a Filipino citizen, and therefore we cannot be sent."

If Matt were to become a U.S. citizen, then of course they would be approved to work under this mission agency.

Out of nearly 170 mission agencies operating in the Philippines, this denomination ranks in the top 10 in terms of personnel. Its total missions budget for 1989 exceeded $15 million.[3]

Looking at the level of involvement in this mission field, it appears that the agency has invested a considerable amount in winning the Philippines for Christ, both in terms of people and finances.

My question is this: If there is a simpler, more efficient and more logical approach to reaching Filipinos with the gospel, why is this agency resisting it? Tragically, all that stands between its ability to multiply its outreach is a man-made policy.

A good fund-raiser. Since the average North American missionary must raise about $43,000 a year in one way or another to go abroad, mission boards must choose candidates who possess excellent public relations and fund-raising skills. Even so-called faith missionaries who cannot directly appeal for funds must spend a large amount of their time speaking and traveling in order to assist in the fund-raising process. The same applies to denominational missionaries who are salaried and don't directly raise support.

And we must assume fund-raising skills will be more important than ever as we approach A.D. 2000, when it could likely take more than $75,000 a year to keep a Western missionary on the field.

These six man-made standards for missionary qualification have gained such widespread use that they obscure some of the most important determining factors that are truly biblical and should be paramount.

These factors include — but are not limited to — soul-winning abilities, church-planting skills, past witnessing experiences, spiritual gifts and calling, and an established life of faith and sacrifice.

The selection process for essential qualities such as these is surprisingly informal in many mission boards. It is not unusual to find missionaries overseas who have demonstrated few spiritual gifts or who have not proven themselves to be effective in local-church ministry in the homeland.

If a missionary candidate is not already a soul-winner and disciple-maker at home, how will going overseas change him? If he has not already established a congregation from scratch in the homeland, why would we think this brother will be a church planter overseas in an alien culture where he doesn't know the language?

The Popular Definition of Today's Missionary

Using the popular criteria now in use, a reasonable definition of a missionary today could be stated something like this: A young, healthy, degreed, mentally stable, well-financed, middle-class North American from a conservative, evangelical Protestant tradition willing to travel abroad to offer technological skills to existing Third World native churches.

Conservative evangelicals especially may take offense at this description, which they may feel is an unfair stereotype, but statistically it matches up to reality more times than not. And it applies to evangelical missions as well as to so-called liberal denominations.

With this kind of popular definition in vogue, it is no surprise that so many in the sending churches do not see or understand the importance of the fast-rising native missionary movement.

Native missionaries, although they are currently doing the New Testament work of missions more effectively than their Western counterparts, are not considered qualified by the most important Western standards.

Western missionary qualifications tend to perpetuate the culture, education, health, science and technology of the West. They make second-class citizens out of God's first-class servants on the mission field. And the use of these false standards guarantees that this mind-set will continue to control the missionary enterprise.

It is no wonder, then, that otherwise qualified, effective native missionaries can so easily be made to appear untrained and unacceptable to Western donors. (By the way, this is why native missionary activity is so under-reported in the Western press. It also reflects why the number of native missionaries appears much smaller than it really is in so many field surveys.)

But aren't there thousands of Western missionaries who love, respect and want to help native missions? Of course there are, and they face a tremendous challenge.

They must go back to their mission boards and home churches and work for changes in the system — changes that will find new and creative ways to free up prayer and financial support for native missionaries. There is really only one practical way to show our love and respect for the ministries of native missionaries: We must start using our mission support structures to send them to the unreached people.

"But whoso hath this world's good, and seeth his brother have need, and shutteth up his bowels of compassion from him, how dwelleth the love of God in him?" (1 John 3:17).

Should We Call Native Missionaries by Another Title?

What I am saying does not always make me very popular in some mission circles. Recently I made one of my frequent trips to Wheaton, Illinois, calling on friends there whom I love and respect.

Wheaton is an affluent college town — upper-middle-class by American standards — with many outstanding Christian organizations.

One warmhearted Wheaton College student, trying to be helpful to me after I had finished my calls in the area, asked if he could drive me back to O'Hare Field to catch my next flight. I thanked him for his servant spirit, and we set off enjoying a good time of sharing about world evangelism.

As we talked I could sense he was living every day under a powerful challenge to go overseas as a traditional missionary and knew firsthand the strong appeal many Western missions are making to young Americans today.

He had read my book *The Coming Revolution in World Missions* and had given it some thought. As we rode along, he turned to me and said sincerely, "K.P., your problems would be over in Wheaton if you just stopped calling your native staff *missionaries*. Can't you call them something else?"

What perceptive advice! I realized immediately that this young man understood the problem exactly, even though he was offering me the wrong solution. His advice seemed to crystallize the problem in my mind as never before.

"No!" I exclaimed. "I will not surrender the word *missionary* and allow only North Americans to use it!" I became so engrossed in explaining why that I almost missed the plane.

"By New Testament standards," I said, "native missionaries are just as qualified as Americans or Europeans to be sent to reach the lost. And they're often more effective in other ways. As long as the word *missionary* remains the term Western churches use to describe pioneer evangelists, I will insist that it apply equally to native missionaries as well.

"And," I added, "I also insist that we define the term *missionary* according to the standards of the New Testament in 1 Timothy 3 and Titus 1."

Notes

[1]Samuel Wilson and John Siewert, eds., *Mission Handbook: North American Protestant Missions Overseas — 13th Edition* (Monrovia, Calif.: MARC, 1986), p. 66.

[2]Article by Roberta Winter and Richard Cotten, "What About National Missionaries?" *Global Prayer Digest* (Pasadena, Calif.: Frontier Fellowship Inc., July 1990).

[3]W. Dayton Roberts and John A. Siewert, eds., *Mission Handbook: USA/Canada Protestant Ministries Overseas — 14th Edition* (Grand Rapids, Mich.: Zondervan Publishing House, 1989), pp. 124, 381.

---------------------------- 8 ----------------------------

The Biblical Definition
of a Missionary

Though we daily use the term *missionary*, I confess that more than once I have seriously contemplated throwing out the word completely. After all, the words *mission* and *missionary* are not even found in the English Bible. Moreover, their meanings have become so muddled in everyday usage that the words almost always need to be coupled with an adjective to make clear what you really mean.

But since most Christians still use *missions* whenever they describe outreach to a lost world — and there is no other equally generic term — it's probably best to retain the word and try to revive its original meaning.

Although the Bible does not actually use the word, the concept of missions is on every page from Genesis to Revelation. The Bible itself is a missionary anthology, a record of messages from the "sending God" of Psalm 67. He is a loving God who reaches out to a race of lost and rebellious sinners. When you define the concept of missions in this biblical context, it takes on a richer meaning.[1] As we do so, I believe we can restore and revive the original meaning, at least among active Christians who still use the word to describe the outreach work of the church.

The Old Testament is full of missionary examples — "sent ones" — from Abel and Noah to Jonah and the prophets. The New Testament gives us a much better picture of missionary calling and work as we understand it today. Here missionaries and their tasks are described in elaborate detail, giving us a very clear picture of how the Lord intends His body on earth to carry out the missionary mandate.

The Lord Jesus as Master Missionary

The best examples of real missionaries in the New Testament are seen in the lives of the first apostles. They learned "Missionary Principles and Practices 101" at the feet of Jesus — the master missionary.

There is no better place, therefore, to begin studying a New Testament missionary definition than in the life of our Lord Jesus Himself. The Lord, who founded the church and gave us our missionary marching orders, was in fact the first missionary in the New Testament sense. "As my Father hath sent me, even so send I you," He said in John 20:21. He best models for us the work and message of a New Testament missionary.

In this verse Jesus actually calls Himself a "sent one," or missionary, in the same way we most commonly use the term today. And He is clearly saying here that additional "sent ones" are to be included in His missionary band. These missionaries are to go and do the work of the gospel as He did. How vital it is for us then to do our missionary work as Jesus did His!

There is no doubt from this passage and many others that He consciously modeled the missionary life of a "sent one" for those who would follow in His steps. (The word *apostle*, of course, means "sent one" and is the closest New Testament word we have to our own English equivalent, *missionary*. Both *apostle* and *missionary* share the same primary definition of "one sent with a religious message.")

Since Jesus is to be master missionary, let us look briefly at some of the elements of His missionary life and ministry.

First, *His purpose.* Jesus gave His own job description in Luke 19:10: "For the Son of man is come to seek and to save that which was lost." He describes Himself as the good Shepherd, always searching to reconcile rebellious mankind to the Father in heaven.

There was an urgency to Christ's purpose. In Mark, the Gospel of action, we see Him always moving on to the next village "immediately" or "straightway" because He knew how short His time was. The cross on which He was to suffer was ever before Him. This action adverb, *euthys*, is used forty-two times in Mark.[2]

The instructions of 2 Corinthians 5:18-21 tell how God has passed on Christ's ministry of reconciliation to us so that we are ambassadors as Christ was, restoring men and women to God.

Second, *His message.* It is amazing to me that Jesus is never seen teaching the balanced, wholistic gospel we hear touted in the seminaries of the West today. In His parables and teachings, Jesus was always taking the things of this world and pointing to the next.

It was as if Jesus were always saying, "How can I help you to understand the world I come from — what heaven is like?" As He taught in parables and illustrations, He was always asking, "To what shall I compare heaven?" as if there were really no way His fallen human listeners could envision the next world.

Christ's concept of the kingdom was nonmaterial and invisible. He wanted to bring all men into an eternal kingdom that was "not of this world," as He told Pilate at His judgment (John 18:36).

How different this message is from the Marxist gospel we hear today from the liberation theologians, or its more peaceful predecessor, the social gospel teaching of the last century. Much of Western theology today brings in a worldview that is totally concerned with the here and now of this material world. Jesus was far more concerned with attracting subjects from this world who would follow Him into the next!

Third, *His style.* Jesus identified fully with us. The message of Philippians 2:7-8 is so clear on this subject. He "made himself of no reputation, and took upon him the form of a servant, and was made in the likeness of men: And being found in fashion as a man, he humbled himself, and became obedient unto death, even the death of the cross."

Jesus accommodated Himself to our human condition so fully that even the most fearful sinner need not be threatened by the message or the messenger, coming as a mere baby, then as a servant — a carpenter. Though King of kings, He came not through armies and government. Though high priest, He came not on the glorious temple mount in Jerusalem. Though He owned the cattle on a thousand hills, He came not among the rich. He chose instead to minister as a homeless wanderer, leading a life of simplicity and poverty.

Jesus chose a missionary style that incarnated the gospel. He didn't just preach the kingdom of God: *He was the kingdom of God.* He didn't just preach the gospel: He was the gospel. Jesus was the first "living epistle," as Paul would later describe believers. "I am the way, the truth, and the life," said Jesus; "no man cometh unto the Father, but by me" (John 14:6).

Paul seemed to understand this incarnation principle well. He so incorporated the concept into his life-style that he was able to tell the church at Corinth to "be...followers of me, even as I also am of Christ" (1 Cor. 11:1). This is the highest standard of consistent living imaginable. To Jesus, Paul and the New Testament missionaries, the gospel was never an intellectual concept; it was a way of life.

Fourth, *His method.* Jesus preferred to teach His missionary band by formation rather than lecture and explanation. Although He frequently paused to answer questions in times of didactic dialogue, He preferred to teach by example — living out each lesson before them.

Most of the time He taught them by example how to be missionaries. As they went from village to village with Jesus, they observed Him doing exactly what He had commanded them: "Heal the sick, cleanse the lepers, raise the dead, cast out devils" (Matt. 10:8).

In this sense Jesus apprenticed His disciples as missionaries rather than provided formal training in a classroom setting.

As He eventually sent them out to proclaim the gospel by themselves, we see that they learned from their own successes and failures. They learned to extend the kingdom of God through miracles and anointed proclamation.

Most of all, Jesus showed them that they needed to abide in Him just as He abided in God the Father. Missionary service is based on intimate resting in God. Only as we rely on God to do the work is the task accomplished, for it is not our work, but His!

Fifth, *His utter submission and obedience unto death.* Jesus refused to contemplate anything less than a life of total submission to God. He chose to live a life without options. "For I came down from heaven, not to do mine own will, but the will of him that sent me" (John 6:38).

Jesus opened His hands voluntarily to the nails of the cross. He accepted a life of scorn and rejection. He understood that obedience to the Father's will would mean a life of suffering and sacrifice and, ultimately, death.

No missionary can have the authority of God resting on his ministry unless, as Jesus, he totally sells out to God. Jesus loved God more than His own life, and He was willing to die in order to save the lost humanity "God so loved...that he gave his only begotten son" (John 3:16).

The disciples caught this same sacrificial zeal. They had been with Jesus. They absorbed His passion for souls and went out to preach the kingdom until they too died martyrs' deaths.

Defining Our Task Correctly

The modern church has failed to define missionaries correctly because it has failed to define the missionary task according to the Great Commission in Matthew 28:19-20; Mark 16:15; Luke 24:46-49; John 20:21; and Acts 1:8. Instead, we have defined missions, and therefore the missionary, in our own cultural terms.

Instead of submitting to the Lord Jesus, we have relied on our own wisdom and thus allowed the missionary task to be defined as an extension of colonialism, denominationalism, humanism and even materialism.

Missionary definitions can be clear so long as we keep them attached to the Great Commission mandate. If we stand by this simple New Testament description of our spiritual warfare, we can readily adapt to any new weapons and strategies needed to carry on the battle in this dawn of the twenty-first century.

The task of the local church is not to serve as a missionary sending agency but as a cell in the universal body of Christ. It is that universal or whole body of Christ which must accomplish the Great Commission in unified cooperation. The "Go ye" of the Great Commission is a command *given in the plural* to the whole body of Christ. It must not be understood in the singular, given only to our local church, denomination or parachurch organization.

As we work together in this way, we will no longer feel the compulsion to send a member from our own congregation or denomination to the "uttermost parts." In fact, we will drop the notion that a true missionary has to be sent from "here" to "there." We are free to join with others and send missionaries from "there" to "there" if that is the more efficient way to use our resources.

And, of course, we will no longer insist that the missionary meet the peculiar qualifications and artificial standards of our local culture, favorite doctrines and denominational traditions.

Instead, we should be able to accept and support any needy missionary from anywhere in the body of Christ. This definition is free from racial, sectarian and vocational overtones. It allows us to help available native missionaries accomplish the task in an effective, efficient manner.

Let us look instead for any "sent one" who is going into all the world to reach those who have not heard the gospel. We will know an authentic missionary because he is like the Lord Jesus. He is preaching the gospel and is a living personification of the message being preached. The sure evidence of this authentic missionary is the trail of living churches that are established in his wake.

Notes

[1]Articles by John R.W. Stott, "The Bible in World Perspective" and "The Living God Is a Missionary God," *Perspectives on the World Christian Movement* (Pasadena, Calif.: William Carey Library, 1981), pp. 3-18. (Also see other articles in Section I, "The Biblical Perspective," pp. 19-127.)

[2]John Walvoord and Roy Zuck, editors, *The Bible Knowledge Commentary — Mark* (Wheaton, Ill.: Victory Books, 1983), p. 105.

9

What Does a True Missionary Do?

The Chinese street vendors didn't even look up as a thin, scholarly looking youth emerged from the gates of the enclave reserved by the emperor for the "green-eyed devils" of the foreign community in Shanghai. He wore Chinese spectacles and shuffled along quickly on his urgent assignment, carrying a precious bag of literature and books.

His shaved head and long black pigtail, as well as the baggy silk pantaloons and teacher's robe, hid an amazing fact. This Chinese-looking doctor wearing flat-soled shoes with turned-up toes was Hudson Taylor, a daring young missionary recruit who was determined to do what everyone said could not be done. He was going to take the gospel of Christ inland, up the rivers from China's port cities and into the forbidden provinces where no white man or evangelist had ever gone before.

Actually a sandy-haired Yorkshire, England, boy barely twenty-one years old, Taylor had given up everything, including the woman he loved, to sail for China and frontier evangelism in the Orient. Out of his patient obedience to the Lord would eventually emerge the great China Inland Mission, the largest of all the colonial missions, and one of the most successful evangelistic bands of all time.

Driven by a passionate zeal for "a million a month dying without God," the impoverished youth was scorned and ridiculed by the older missionaries who greeted him in Shanghai. His poverty, lack of education, refusal of ordination and insistence on identification with the Chinese were not amusing or commendable to others in the carefully watched foreign community.

Starting in 1854, and for many years thereafter, Hudson Taylor was to be an embarrassment to them — a dangerous fool who risked his own life and the lives of others to press into forbidden regions and preach the gospel where Christ had not been named.

But Taylor had a spiritual secret. He would submit as Jesus did to the way of the cross. "Not I, but Christ" was the motto that would keep him moving and organizing a militant task-force of gospel teachers.

He was willing to take the risks to follow his Lord into the remote provinces and villages of the Chinese interior. When it came time for him to join his Savior fifty-one years later, he was preceded in death by nearly two hundred who had joined CIM and were martyred by the Chinese for trying to bring the gospel inland. Hundreds of others, including wives and children, died of exotic fevers and the harsh life of travel. Although these itinerant evangelists knew the rigors and risks of the mobile life-style he demanded, they also were willing to pay the price. After all, it was the souls of the Chinese which were at stake: "...more than 1,000 every hour are passing away into death and darkness."[1]

Hudson Taylor's Zeal for the Lost

Missiologist Ralph Winter says, "God strangely honored him because his gaze was fixed upon the world's least reached people. Hudson Taylor had a divine wind behind him. It took 20 years for other missions to begin to join Taylor in his special emphasis — the unreached, inland frontiers."[2]

The missionary life and ministry of Hudson Taylor are marked by four impressive achievements: (1) He did the work of a missionary as defined by the Lord Jesus. (2) He proclaimed the New Testament missionary message. (3) He paved the way for authentic, indigenous churches. (4) He developed and possessed an inner life that reflected the missionary life-style of Jesus.

We cannot address the question "What does a true missionary do?" unless our answer includes these four basic elements.

And, of course, as we now must consider supporting a fresh army of native missionaries who will take us into the twenty-first century, we want to send out only those who bear these precious earmarks of servanthood to Christ.

The Lord's Missionary Job Description

If your letter-carrier arrived at the door one day and, instead of delivering the mail, asked to come in and fix the sink, you would know something was very wrong at the post office. That's exactly the situation in Christian missions today, and almost no one is stopping to ask why.

In many cases the job descriptions of modern North American missionaries bear little resemblance to the relevant scriptures defining true missionary activity. And because many don't know what they should be doing, they are not able to evaluate their work honestly.

The problem is that the churches and missions which send them don't know how to hold missionaries accountable to their calling. As a result we face a genuine crisis in identifying the missionary task. The time has come when we must be honest with ourselves — asking what exactly has gone wrong and what we can do to correct the error.

Jesus Christ could not have made the Great Commission clearer than He did in Matthew 28:19-20: "Go ye therefore, and teach all nations, baptizing them in the name of the Father, and of the Son, and of the Holy Ghost: teaching them to observe all things whatsoever I have commanded you...."

In this passage, the job description of the missionary is clear. In four other places in the New Testament we find the same mission statement elaborated. The task of the missionary is simply to *convert and disciple nations to Christ.*

Too many of our missions have substituted their own human genius for obedience. "That can't be how Jesus would say it today," goes their interpretation. "He knows that villages need wells, babies need milk powder and unjust economic orders must be overturned — so instead we'll dig wells, but we'll just dig them in the name of Jesus."

The gospel these modern missionaries preach is usually not articulated in words, since their theology often avoids clearly proclaiming any kind of message. Digging the well and supplying humanitarian aid is considered a "witness" that speaks for itself. They vaguely hope that through such activity people will somehow come to understand their message, which often goes something like "God loves you, and we do too." While the children of this world surely need to hear and know that God loves them, such a statement is a distortion of truth without the rest of the gospel. God has called His church not only to serve people but also to preach "all the counsel of God" (Acts 20:27).

Unfortunately, social programs are often the only "gospel" left behind by those who have captured control of so many mission agencies and programs from the West. Unlike those missionaries dedicated to preaching the whole gospel, their actions do nothing to change lives or restore people to a right relationship with God.

No wonder these "change society" mission strategies have made so little impact on lives after nearly 150 years on almost every mission field. Millions of dollars are still being spent annually on this "half-gospel" — which is really no gospel at all, but rather a bandage on the gaping wounds of sin and rebellion.

Their substitute for the Great Commission is a deception cooked up by the god of this world. Satan's half-truths often cause guilt and even compassion. Yet this lie has caused millions to believe that meeting physical needs is somehow equated with preaching the gospel of Christ.

Regrettably, many missions today are doing just about everything to help the human race *except* preaching and making disciples. It's far easier to be sent to the mission field today if you're an ecologist, lawyer, musician, teacher or broadcast technician rather than a preacher or church planter.

Five Tasks of a Missionary

During His earthly ministry, Jesus set an example for the disciples of five specific missionary tasks. By breaking them down into their parts, we get a much clearer idea of what Jesus really meant missionary work to be all about.

(1) *Preach the gospel of the kingdom* (Matt. 10:7; Mark 3:14; Mark 16:15; Luke 9:2; Luke 9:60; Acts 5:42; Acts 16:10; Acts 17:3; Rom. 15:20; 1 Cor. 1:23; 2 Cor. 4:5; Gal. 1:9).

The emphasis is always on announcing the arrival of Jesus as the messianic Savior. By the end of each Gospel, there is no longer any doubt that the gospel of Christ refers to a spiritual, heavenly kingdom rather than an earthly one. In fact, whenever the disciples pushed Jesus to inaugurate an earthly kingdom, He put them off. The priority of the Lord was elsewhere. The invisible world is recognized as superior and separate from the material kingdoms of this earth in Christ's gospel, and the good news He preached invited mankind to be part of it. So the gospel we preach first must seek to reconcile men and women to God rather than create a new world order. It looks toward a kingdom coming in eternity.

(2) *Baptize* (Matt. 3:11; Matt. 28:19; Luke 3:16; John 1:33; Acts 2:38-41; Acts 8:38; Acts 10:47-48; Acts 16:33).

By putting the emphasis on baptism, Jesus made sure the disciples would clearly be calling people to repentance and conversion. In the waters of baptism we unmistakably make a conscious break with past religion and life-style, declaring allegiance to Jesus. As we act out the drama of salvation in the waters of baptism, it is an unforgettable way to declare explicitly our death to past sin and the new beginning of life in Christ.

(3) *Teach and disciple* (Matt. 4:23; Matt. 26:55; Matt. 28:20; Mark 6:34; Luke 13:22; Acts 5:42; Acts 15:35; 1 Cor. 4:17; Col. 1:28; Col. 3:16; 2 Tim. 2:2).

The emphasis here is on training and instilling a new way of life into kingdom converts. No wonder, then, that Jesus spent three years living this life-style before the disciples. As they lived with Him and imitated His life, they were unconsciously learning how to model their new life-style to other converts. And it worked. People knew by the way they acted and talked that they had been with the Nazarene.

(4) *Cast out demons* (Matt. 8:16; Matt. 10:1; Mark 1:27; Mark 3:11; Luke 4:36; Luke 9:1; Luke 10:17).

Missionary work is spiritual warfare against the powers of darkness that hold men and women captive to sin. Missionaries are expected to use the authority Christ has given them in "casting down imaginations, and every high thing that exalteth itself against the knowledge of God" (2 Cor. 10:5). Jesus was routinely acknowledged as Lord by evil spirits, and He taught His disciples to take authority over them as He did.

(5) *Heal the sick* (Matt. 4:24; Matt. 9:6; Matt. 10:8; Matt. 14:14; Mark 2:11; Mark 6:56; Mark 16:18; Acts 5:15-16; James 5:14-15).

Obviously Jesus wasn't talking about modern medicine here. He didn't tell His missionaries to open clinics and operate hospitals. Instead, He gave them the Holy Spirit so that they would share His power and authority to heal the sick. Of course, this doesn't mean medical ministry is wrong, but it does reveal that Jesus is making His healing power available to all His followers as they minister in His name.

In short, these New Testament missionaries were nothing less than agents of divine reconciliation and redemption. They followed in the steps of Christ. They walked as He walked, talked as He talked and carried on the work He came to do. Anything more or less than the above cannot qualify as authentic New Testament missionary work. At best it might be argued that other kinds of modern-day mission activities might *assist* evangelists and indigenous churches to reach their nations. But the Lord obviously expected a lot more out of the disciples He commissioned. And the actual New Testament record, as well as the history of the church since, shows that great church growth is accomplished when missionaries move with New Testament power and authority.

The superficial add-ons of most modern mission movements actually have hindered rather than helped the spread of the gospel and the church — no matter how wonderful they sound in fund-raising appeals.

Nowhere do we see this more clearly than in the history of Chinese missions. In pre-revolutionary China, most historians estimate the size of the church in 1949 to have been from three million to five million souls. But, despite their small size, Christian missions in China then operated a large network of mission schools and hospitals — perhaps more extensive there than on any other mission field. In addition there were Christian newspapers, publishing houses and a large infrastructure of influential parachurch organizations.

After the communist revolution these institutions were confiscated, and the foreign missionaries who operated them were deported. Under communist persecution the Chinese church was forced to worship underground and become indigenous. It was purged of all ability to offer materialistic ministries and thus forced to return to the basic task of preaching and teaching the gospel in small-group settings.

The results have stunned the mission world. Today, despite bloody persecution, the church in China is considered to be at least ten times the size it was before the revolution. Most estimates vary from thirty million to seventy million, and responsible authorities believe it to be around fifty million. Even the communist-dominated Three Self Patriotic

Movement churches have grown dramatically. By rediscovering the correct emphasis on New Testament priorities rather than becoming preoccupied with institutions and social services, the church has actually grown faster and stronger than it did under foreign missionary control.

The lesson is obvious. True missionaries concentrate on doing the work of Mark 16:15 rather than dissipating their energies operating social-welfare programs. True missionaries serve the message of Christ, not the institutions of the church.

The Message of the Missionary

Four elements characterize this gospel message, and Jesus touched on them all in the quotation of the Great Commission in Luke 24:44-49.

First, *it is centered on the messianic person of Christ.* His coming with the gospel was foreshadowed and predicted in the Law of Moses and the Prophets, says Jesus in verse 44. The missionary message is the good news that God loves lost humanity and is establishing a new order under the leadership and direction of His Son.

The first missionaries were caught up with the person of Christ. They had discovered not just the gospel but the Lord of the gospel. This was Emmanuel — God with us. "Thou art the Son of God," exclaims Nathanael as he confesses Christ as Messiah (John 1:49).

"We have found the Messiah," shouts an excited Andrew to Peter in John 1:41. From the beginning it was impossible to separate Christ Himself from His message. He personified the gospel of God's love. The whole of the Old Testament history looks forward to Christ, and the whole of the New Testament centers around Him.

Second, *the real gospel always deals with the forgiveness of sin.* Jesus says in Luke 24:46-47 that He had to suffer, die and rise from the dead for the "remission of sins." The real gospel is a gospel of atonement.

Jesus knew that injustice, crime, sickness and poverty were merely the symptoms of our iniquity — not the central problems of it. Jesus never taught that our behavior was the by-product of environment. Jesus understood that iniquity is genetically within our fallen race. The Bible says He knew the inherent sinful heart of man and did not trust it (John 2:24-25; Matt. 15:19).

Jesus came to deal with the root cause of sin by going to the cross. By offering Himself as a blood sacrifice to redeem and reconcile us to God,

He made it possible for us to overcome sin and enter into the kingdom of God.

Third, *the real gospel message always deals with a call to repentance.* Jesus says in Luke 24:47 that "repentance...should be preached in his name among all nations, beginning at Jerusalem."

There was never anything in the life of Christ, in the message of Christ or in the New Testament that cheapened the grace of God and made the gospel easy to accept. Although salvation was a gift of God purchased for us with His own blood, Jesus made it uncomfortably clear that those who desired to follow Him must do so with their entire lives.

Jesus, as He dealt personally with would-be converts, put His finger on the idols in their lives. Nothing that stood between Jesus and His disciples was tolerated. He demanded that each believer take up his or her cross and follow Him, dying to self. Ego-trips are not allowed in the kingdom of heaven.

The gospel message is a call to discipleship and obedience. It requires nothing less than a spiritual U-turn at the cross of Christ. Unless one repents and is born again as a follower of Christ, the spiritual transaction of the gospel has not taken place.

Fourth, *the real gospel message is presented with power and authority.* In Luke 24:49, Jesus commands His disciples to wait before preaching the gospel until they have been "endued with power from on high."

The message of the missionary is not understood primarily on the intellectual level, but is "the living word," to be proclaimed through God's power. The Lord has promised to back up this proclamation with miraculous signs, wonders and other evidences of His divine presence in the message and the messenger. When this power is in operation, it has the wondrous ability to change lives, restore families, heal broken hearts and free the oppressed from addiction and bondage.

Notes

[1]Dr. and Mrs. Howard Taylor, *J. Hudson Taylor: God's Man in China* (Chicago, Ill.: Moody Press, 1978), p. 272.

[2]Article by Ralph D. Winter, "The Long Look: Eras of Missions History," *Perspectives on the World Christian Movement* (Pasadena, Calif.: William Carey Library, 1981), p. 172.

The Key: Indigenous Church Planting

I n the book of Acts and throughout the rest of the New Testament, the work of the first missionaries becomes preoccupied with Christ's command to make disciples. This was done through starting local churches, usually made up of what we might today call a network of home Bible studies. "They [continued] daily with one accord in the temple, and breaking bread from house to house...praising God" (Acts 2:46-47a).

These simple house meetings were the first indigenous churches. They were the clear evidence of successful missionary work — house groups that served as spiritual incubators in which the Lord was able to form a living, separated, witnessing body within the larger secular community.

In a few mission agencies this is being recognized, and there are calls for a return to church planting. However, the tragedy in many Western missions today is that church planting among unreached people groups is barely even mentioned in planning strategies. The latest statistics from the fourteenth edition of the *Mission Handbook* provide little evidence there has been a change in the situation.

You can attend great mission conferences, and the subject will barely be addressed. For example, in 1989 at the Lausanne II Congress on World Evangelization in Manila, not one plenary session was devoted to the planting of local churches.

No wonder more than two-thirds of Western missionaries today can't make a direct link between what they do and a growing body of believers.

But, according to the Great Commission, any so-called missionary activity which does not contribute to the growth of the church is simply unbiblical. Such outreach usually results in spiritual malnourishment and a lack of true unity among believers.

When we give birth to physical babies, we wouldn't think of leaving them in the street to survive by themselves — so why should we do this in the spiritual realm? Missions which do not give birth to a local church are ineffective; they do not go far enough in fulfilling the Great Commission which instructs us to make disciples of the nations and teach them to observe all the Lord commands. Mission organizations that do not build local churches drain billions of dollars (and over two-thirds of all Western missionaries) away from effective disciple-making ministries that are building the church. Such unscriptural efforts are probably one of the greatest blights on mission work today.

A simple reading of the New Testament proves that the Lord Jesus longs for missionaries to be primarily concerned with church start-ups. The whole New Testament, in fact, is practically a church planter's handbook.

In Acts 2 the Holy Spirit fell on the assembled believers at Jerusalem, and the apostles immediately moved out into the streets to obey the commands of the Great Commission. As a result of these open-air meetings, thousands turned to Christ. Within days the church began to form as they were meeting in the synagogue and from house to house.

As the missionaries went from city to city calling on Jews and then Gentiles to recognize Jesus, we find the new converts gathered immediately into groups for teaching, communion and worship. Because of persecution from the Jews and then the Romans, many of these house fellowships met almost as underground groups. Thus, the first local congregations exploded into existence in city after city without church buildings, schools, hospitals or other institutional ministries.

This first missionary work was so effective that within a few decades the church had spread cross-culturally throughout the entire Roman empire. Hundreds of local ethnic groups and languages heard the gospel. It is fascinating to contemplate that this was done during a time when Christianity was an unregistered, illegal cult which did not enjoy the protection of the Roman government.

The books of the New Testament concern themselves almost entirely with the work undertaken to disciple the first groups of believers, define doctrines for them, establish codes of Christian conduct and prepare them as the bride of Christ for His soon return.

When we begin to understand the New Testament in these terms, it is difficult to comprehend how mission policies and strategy could have gotten so sidetracked. One explanation might be that Western missions have somehow been deliberately sabotaged by a satanic plot.

Most Western missionaries who go overseas as social workers do so under a philosophy that says they intend to "minister both physically and spiritually." Unfortunately, without a clear goal of making converts and planting churches, many find themselves swamped by an ocean of physical need.

Sadly, some have gone to extremes and adopted a theological system that encourages this separation of the spiritual from the material and enthrones physical needs above spiritual.

But even when we have missions which place the priority on making converts and planting churches, we find that many still get tripped up on the next logical question: *What kind of church will it be?* Will we plant indigenous churches, or should they follow the free-form style of American religion with strong, entrepreneurial lay leaders? Will they be Congregational, Episcopalian or Presbyterian in polity? Will they seek to be strongly separated from government as the church is in the United States, or will they seek to be protected by secular authority as the historic state churches in Western Europe?

Besides structural questions, the sensitive Western missionary must decide if he will allow an indigenous theological system to develop or propagate one of the great systems of the West, such as Calvinism, Catholicism, Pentecostalism, Wesleyanism and the like.

What Is an Indigenous Church?

The answers to these and many other questions about the churches we launch also are answered by looking to the examples of church planting by the first missionaries. Please note that this is not meant to advocate primitivism. Such utopian attempts to recreate a church caste in New Testament cultural terms no more lead to indigenous churches than does any other polity that imitates past tradition. However, the student of missions must look there for basic principles. We must begin our quest for an authentic indigenous church by asking, What were the characteristics of the first indigenous churches planted by New Testament missionaries?

First, *they were centered on Christ and the gospel*. One cannot imagine the New Testament apostles building the church around anything but the Lord Himself: "For other foundation can no man lay than that is laid, which is Jesus Christ" (1 Cor. 3:11). They did not build churches around "brand-name" denominations, creeds, statements of faith or doctrinal fads as some missionaries do today. It is interesting that Paul and the New Testament writers simply refer to churches by location, such as the church at Corinth, the church at Ephesus and so forth.

Nor did the apostles build the church around particular leaders, human personalities or any other division, such as a particular system of ecclesiastical government, language, mode of baptism, method of celebrating communion, race or social class. All these divisions have been added through the years by accidents of history, prejudices and the teachings of various theologians — some half-wrong and some half-right.

Because of these traditions, much of today's mission activity is not church planting at all, but the export of denominational doctrinal divisions and cults that have already split the churches of Europe and North America. In a very real sense this mission work is not spreading *the* gospel but "another gospel" and "another Jesus" as Paul described in Galatians 1:6-7 and 2 Corinthians 11:4.

Second, *they tried to build a culturally neutral church*. The early missionaries debated long and hard about whether to require Gentile converts to adopt the Jewish customs and laws they loved and grew up with in their synagogues. Many sincerely believed new converts to Christianity should become culturally Jewish — and they had some powerful Old Testament arguments for their belief. Finally, however, the Holy Spirit had His way, and they chose to allow the new converts to remain as free as possible from the foreign influences of Judaism (Acts 15:1-29). We can only wish that all modern missionaries would follow this same New Testament wisdom and consciously avoid mixing their cultural norms with evangelism.

The apostolic decision to leave the Gentiles culturally free paved the way for the local churches to develop customs and standards relevant to their own cultures. The New Testament remains wonderfully silent on most of the specific issues that have divided the Western church over the years! This principle should help us form policies that leave mission field congregations free to evolve their own interpretations and practice on nonessentials. No matter how much the missionary loves the familiar songs, symbols and creeds under which he was raised, they must be detached from the essential gospel he presents on the field.

Bruce Britten shares an African viewpoint of this truth: "Today many Africans in central and southern Africa are saying, 'We see that God planned for us to receive faith in Christ, but must we also follow the foreign customs which the missionaries brought?'

"Professor B. Makhathini of the University of Swaziland gave the following excellent answer:

" 'Before the bread of life (the Christian faith) came to our part of Africa, it stayed in Europe for over a thousand years. There the Europeans added a plastic bag (their own customs) to the bread. And when they came to southern Africa, they fed us the plastic bag along with the bread. Now the plastic is making us sick! The plastic is theirs. But the bread belongs to everyone. We know that God planned for us to receive the bread just as He planned for them to receive it. We can remove the plastic and enjoy the bread.' "[1]

Too often missionaries unconsciously train new converts to follow imported policies and practices without considering local customs. No missionary activity should ever impose a foreign system of church government, liturgy, vestments or even technologies upon new converts. These cultural and historical attachments to the Christian faith are almost always of a fleshly or worldly nature. While they might have had some logical justification when first developed in Canterbury, Philadelphia, Nashville, Rome or Springfield, that doesn't mean they should be exported to the mission field.

Outside of their original place and time in history, most foreign church laws and policies simply don't transfer to the mission field. Overseas, they only serve to build greater barriers between the local Christians and their neighbors. Through their use by missionaries and denominational leaders, the local church gains a reputation of being more alien than it is, and her witness to the larger community becomes increasingly difficult.

Paul's principle of cultural accommodation is stated in 1 Corinthians 9:19-22: "For though I be free from all men, yet have I made myself servant unto all, that I might gain the more. And unto the Jews I became as a Jew, that I might gain the Jews; to them that are under the law, as under the law, that I might gain them that are under the law; to them that are without law, as without law, (being not without law to God, but under the law to Christ,) that I might gain them that are without law. To the weak became I as weak, that I might gain the weak: I am made all things to all men, that I might by all means save some."

Third, *New Testament missionaries built a morally separated church.* Paul rarely wrote an epistle without making practical applications to everyday living. Romans 12-15, Galatians 5-6, Ephesians 4-6, Philippians 4 and Colossians 3-4 are chapters that reveal the heart of the Lord for a pure and spotless bride. Christians are clearly to be different, but not in superficial cultural terms. The distinguishing mark of any true believer is holiness.

The New Testament word *ecclesia* for our "church" means "a calling out" — and implies separation from the world. True missionaries are preparing the church described in Revelation 21, a bride adorned for her husband.

Fourth, *the New Testament church was self-supporting, self-propagating and self-governing.* Indigenous churches didn't begin with the "three self" movement of the mid-1850s. The first missionaries planted "three self" churches as naturally as breathing.

The apostles never "colonized" their converts or built an imperial system that taxed local congregations or linked them formally to a distant headquarters. These political-power issues seldom appear in the New Testament record. In fact, the first missionaries often made a point of offering the gospel without charge as we read in Acts 3:6; 18:3; 1 Corinthians 4:12 and 9:18. They were either supported by the believers who had sent them or worked with their own hands at trades in order to give the gospel without charge.

Paul and the apostles, like Jesus before them, authenticated their missionary authority over the churches they founded on the basis of their sacrifice and suffering for the believers. By the moral weight of their proven servant spirits, they had already earned their leadership.

Which leads us to the last and most important characteristic of what a genuine missionary is: *one who leads by example a consistent Christian life*. This involves the missionary in the ministry of incarnating Christ's servanthood to the church.

The Missionary as an Example of Christ

"Christ...loved the church, and gave himself for it," says Ephesians 5:25. It comes as no surprise, then, to discover that true missionary work demands that the disciple care for the church as Jesus does. The missionary follows the example of Christ, whose love for the church Paul likened to that of the husband in marriage.

The missionary call is not a career or vocation as such, but a life-style based on displaying the genuine concern of Christ for the welfare of His church. The decision to live and walk in this reality cannot be made without total commitment. There is no such thing as a part-time missionary — even if one is temporarily doing tentmaking in a bivocational situation.

Every minute of every day the missionary is modeling the life of Christ to his followers. He should be able to say, as Paul did to the Corinthians, "Be ye followers of me, even as I also am of Christ" (1 Cor. 11:1).

The missionary's ethics, habits, finances, personal life and family life are a living object lesson for all to see. Paul, Silvanus and Timothy, a three-member missionary band to Thessalonica, were able to write back and tell the young Christians how to behave — using themselves as examples! In 2 Thessalonians 3:7 we find them saying, "For yourselves know how ye ought to follow us: for we behaved not ourselves disorderly among you."

Sri Lankan missions leader Ajith Fernando, in an exposition of Mark 10:35-45, put his finger on this need for servanthood in the October 1987 issue of *Mission Frontiers*:

"God calls us to identify with our hearers, to become one with them — with their struggles, their aspirations and their experiences. Alas, this seems to be one of the blind spots of American missions. I regret to say this, but I think I need to say it: I believe Americans are possibly the most generous and open-hearted people in the world. They are blessed with a sense of fair play that is unusual in most parts of the world.

"But I fear that there has not been sufficient serious thinking about incarnation, about lifestyle, about what it means to identify. Perhaps it is understandable considering the relative affluence here. Your poor people have much more than most of the people in our countries. So a sacrificial dropping of lifestyle which seems very drastic to an American missionary may still not be enough of an incarnation in poorer nations.

"I fear this is happening a lot today. Not among everyone, but I think there are too many people with a warm heart, with genuine love, but with insufficient identification."[2]

Jesus said, "The son of man came not to be ministered unto, but to minister" (Matt. 20:28). To do this, the real missionary to the Third World must represent Christ in at least four essential areas: obedience, suffering, sacrifice and commitment.

The beautiful story of Rajan and Deva Lal (not their real names) illustrates what it really means to represent the love of Christ.

No family should be asked to pay the price they did to bring the gospel to the lost, but I have never heard a murmur of complaint from them. And they never talk about the deep sacrifices they have made to pioneer their mission to the unreached tribal people of North India.

Brother Rajan first sensed the call of God on his life to leave the rich, beautiful paddy fields of Kerala about twenty-five years ago. Friends and family couldn't believe he would leave his comfort and security for the sake of the animistic tribes of the north. The people there lived on freezing mountainsides, practicing slash-and-burn farming. They were enslaved to alcohol and the worship of demon spirits.

Rajan shared this burden with the leaders of the nominal Christian church in his home village — but they had no money or vision to send a missionary. Even his own pastor advised him not to go and finally refused to help. But Rajan knew God was calling him to go. He didn't know of any mission agency or way to raise funds for such a mission, but he knew he had to go.

After praying for many months, Rajan and Deva both decided to sell all they had and move to the cold and barren hills of the north. It meant learning a new dialect, adapting to a new life-style and patiently working with an illiterate tribal group that was still without a Christian community.

Rajan and Deva were compelled by a supernatural love that they could not explain. When they finally arrived and saw the terrible poverty and ignorance that gripped the mountain people, they were more certain than ever that God had called them to bring Christ and the gospel to these people who had lived in darkness for centuries.

The first few months and years were the hardest. They knew no one, and at first no congregation supported them. Rajan walked from village to village, learning the dialect and sharing Christ.

As the months passed, their money began to run out. At first they skipped a meal each day. Then they would go without meals for a day or two, buying only milk for the children. But soon even that ran out.

As time went by, it became obvious their five year-old was seriously affected by the lack of food. His weak little body was wasting away, and each cold or fever left him weaker than the last.

They prayed and called out to God, but there just wasn't any money to provide the boy with the diet he needed to recover. One day Rajan came home to find Deva weeping beside the still form of their firstborn son. He had slipped quietly into eternity, his tiny body too weak to face the rigors of life on that barren mountain countryside.

Rajan and Deva knew that thousands of starving Indian children die daily from diseases brought on by malnutrition, but why their boy? Weren't they the servants of God? Undoubtedly, back on the rich plains of Kerala, with family and friends, the child would have lived — but they knew God had called them to the people of these mountains. Could God really have wanted their little boy as a price for evangelizing the tribes?

The question had no answer. So they prayed and buried the boy's little body — offering him back to the Lord. Rajan could only comfort his grieving wife with the words of Paul in Colossians 1:24 when he said he rejoiced in his sufferings because they "fill up that which is behind of the afflictions of Christ in my flesh for his body's sake, which is the church."

Today the Lals have a wonderful ministry with a large evangelistic team of over thirty native missionaries reaching many different tribes. Gospel for Asia has been able to take on their support with the help of sponsors in the United States — and every child in their mission is now getting a balanced diet.

But without their faithfulness during those months and years of hunger, loneliness and sacrifice, there would be no work among the tribal people of that particular state today. Rajan and Deva are not unusual. Throughout the Third World today there are thousands of unknown missionary couples and singles like them. They are dedicated men and women who have voluntarily chosen to risk hunger, stonings, persecution and rejection in order to bring Christ to people groups still without a gospel witness. They are the ones the book of Hebrews identifies as heroes of the faith — the ones described as those "of whom the world was not worthy" (Heb. 11:38).

As Paul wrote in Philippians 3:10, these native missionaries have chosen to know "the fellowship of his sufferings, being made conformable unto his death."

What then does a true missionary do? For anyone in the Third World today, it starts with a decision to identify totally with Christ. It means being willing to live with the suffering and poverty of unreached people — unselfishly surrendering comforts, security and privacy in order to reach them.

Missionary life and work are ongoing obedience to Christ, submitting to His will daily and incarnating what He would do to reach the twelve thousand unreached people groups still without a witness.

How many of the missionaries we send from the West today are able to fulfill this job description? That is one of the many questions some of our mission agencies and societies no longer want to talk or write about.

In the next chapter we will raise more questions about the state of Western missions that must be answered in order for us to reach the six billion population of our world by A.D. 2000.

Notes

[1]Bruce Britten, *We Don't Want Your White Religion* (Manzini, Swaziland, 1984), p. 26.

[2]Article by Ajith Fernando, "Servanthood: Jesus' Model for Missions," *Mission Frontiers* (Pasadena, Calif.: U.S. Center for World Mission, October 1987), p. 9.

11

What Missionaries
Don't Talk About

There is a marvelous excitement when your plane touches down in the United States after living and working overseas. Efficiency and effectiveness seem to crackle in the very air Americans breathe. Phones work; clean water runs hot and cold; restrooms smell fresh; food is served appetizingly and hot.

Americans are a people on the go. Pragmatism and technology rule. If it's broken, we fix it now. If it can't be fixed, we replace it. Often a spare part is on the way from some computerized warehouse the same day, delivered the next morning by overnight courier.

Compared to their counterparts overseas, American business and even government institutions are wondrous in the way they realistically measure and evaluate results. Dishonesty is not tolerated for long — if something is unprofitable or inefficient, Americans won't stand in line long before speaking out in protest.

Since they live in a market-driven economy, Americans eventually vote with their feet and pocketbooks, closing down redundant and ineffective organizations.

This efficiency based on sober reality seems almost universal until we look at the way we are now dealing with the current crisis in Christian missions. Suddenly, on this one subject, we're in fantasy land. History, logic and current events go out the window. It sometimes appears as if the last fifty years have not happened. Too often we find ourselves talking with missionaries who act as if we're still back in the days of the British empire.

When it comes to discussing indigenous missions, romantic paternalism often reigns supreme. The conversation loses all touch with reality and is cast in terms of "we" and "them" — and "we" (as in *we the sending church*) always know what's best for "them." And some believers, usually so fair-minded and just, still insist on dealing with indigenous church leaders and missionaries as if they were children.

Too infrequently, if ever, will the typical Western mission leaders talk in terms of an equal partnership with nationals — let alone take the biblical position that Jesus taught, that of becoming a servant to the indigenous leadership.

An Honor Guard of Self-delusion

One of the hardest things for Third World leaders to deal with from Christians in the United States is the century-old wall of sentimentality that stands guard around so many missions programs. Mission leaders have difficulty parting with Western missions programs that are no longer functioning effectively.

Perhaps the hardest part of the puzzle is the attitude of former missionaries who have returned to the United States and sit on boards and committees that control the purse strings of support for indigenous missions and programs overseas.

When these Western mission leaders consistently vote down requests for support by needy native missionaries, we must ask the question of 1 John 3:17, "But whoso hath this world's good, and seeth his brother have need, and shutteth up his bowels of compassion from him, how dwelleth the love of God in him?"

When we quote John 3:16, we must also remember 1 John 3:16: "Hereby perceive we the love of God, because he laid down his life for us: *and we ought to lay down our lives for the brethren*" (italics mine).

Next to the Great Commission, that is the greatest theme verse ever

110

written for *our* global missions outreach. Even as I quote these verses, note that I am deliberately using the term "our missions" in this context. I have chosen that pronoun carefully. These tears and cries from my heart for the state of missions come from one who loves the people and the churches of this wonderful country. I cry out for change in our mission policies as one who identifies as fully as I can with this, my land.

How Long Must Third World Missions Cry Out?

Nothing in this book will come as a particular surprise to knowledgeable mission leaders in the West. The facts of the situation are well-known to key church and mission leaders, but they are too often unwilling to deal with the situation.

This is especially true of my fellow mission leaders, association executives, editors, fund-raising executives, professors and teachers. Privately, most agree that a reformation in missions support policy is long overdue — but they don't want to be the first to speak out.

Meanwhile, we are now looking at the day when fifty-two million people a year will die and slip into eternity — that's one million souls a week by A.D. 2000.[1]

Yet there is some hope that reformation might come, if we will faithfully fan the flames of change. At the 1989 Lausanne II Congress in Manila, knowledgeable observers who have attended international missions conferences for years reported a major change had occurred.

From the platform, native leadership was spoken of in new terms. There was a growing realization that the initiative in world evangelization has slipped from the West into the hands of indigenous missionaries.

However, not everything at Lausanne II reflected the reality of the change. *Christianity Today* noted that "the majority (27 of 43) of the plenary speakers were white Westerners...despite two LCWE consultations in the past two years for the purpose of identifying and encouraging a new generation of worldwide leadership."

Correspondent Lyn Cryderman commented on the dominance of missions by "the old guard," noting that "some questioned whether the (Lausanne) movement is ready or willing to welcome individuals from the Third World or North American minority groups, and if it is serious about passing the torch to a new generation."

However, while the leadership remained dominated by the West in

1989, it was obvious that younger Western leaders were ready to yield the control of missions in the 1990s and beyond to native leaders.

In the workshops, which best represented the frontline activities of missions, indigenous missionary speakers were clearly setting the future agenda to reach the last of "the hidden peoples" and to "evangelize whole nations — with or without the assistance of the West."[2]

But this shift to Third World leadership is no surprise to observers who have been studying developments. Ralph Winter, after the last Asia Missions Association conference, noted in an interview that "we in the West will have a strategic role, but missions in the remaining part of this century will clearly be dominated by the Third World, not the West."

The New Role of the West

And what role does that leave Western churches and missions to play in these new movements? The sole available option is the one offered by Christ Himself — to assist and participate as a servant.

This indispensable supporting role is really the important one left for Western mission agencies who want to be part of the Great Commission in the days ahead. To do so means, of course, a change in heart and attitude that must be deliberate and intentional.

If Western Christian leaders will return to New Testament principles for assisting indigenous missionary movements overseas, it is very likely we could see world evangelization completed in our generation.

And this truth does not apply just to the North American missions community. The churches in Australia, Europe and many other developed nations also can play a valuable role in missions. Just as small nations like the Celts, the Irish, the Spanish and the Portuguese have profoundly impacted world evangelism in the past, there is no reason why missions movements cannot be born anew in nations and places other than North America.

Will Korea, India, Japan or the Philippines rise up with Holy Spirit-empowered vision for a reformation in missions? Perhaps. However, they will be able to fulfill their role only if church and missions leadership changes support policies toward indigenous missions.

But will this change happen in North America? It would be good to report that the necessary attitudes of humility, repentance and servant-hood are prevailing. It would be good to report that Western agencies are using their support-raising networks to support indigenous missions. However, the reality is quite different. Most mission leaders continue to turn a deaf ear to the truth about native missions, blocking funds for their support.

A friend of mine, a veteran of colonial-era missions, has spent over twenty years of his life on the mission field. His comments to me about the lack of servanthood in our Western leaders shed new light on a problem that would be hard to believe were it not for the weight of his experience.

He tells me of some leaders who will say almost anything in order to perpetuate personal power, often using a smoke screen of rumors and untruths to discredit the ministries of native leaders seeking support in the West. Apparently, the ultimate motive for this is a determination to keep the flow of mission dollars and personnel in their own hands. They have been known to malign the character of indigenous mission leaders. They may characterize attempts to support indigenous missions as a violation of "sound indigenous church policy."

Similar to secular businesses and corporations, many denominational mission agencies and independent mission boards employ public relations agents and fund-raisers.

North American agencies and denominations publish over one thousand magazines, newspapers and other publications every month. Tens of thousands of newsletters and appeals for funds flood the mailboxes of Christian homes every month in the United States alone. In addition, news releases, films, videos and special newsletters cover local congregations and church leadership with the missions challenge. Daily mission broadcasts are also heard on virtually every Christian radio and TV station in the United States.

Of course, to raise prayer and support it is necessary to have trained media staff. Unfortunately, a large part of these missions communications programs is focused on maintaining the status quo in missions — even though the programs they defend have continued for decades without honest evaluation.

The Instinct for Self-preservation

Some mission leaders sincerely believe that indigenous missionaries cannot be trusted to do as good a job as white foreigners. The bottom

line of their thinking is basically, My way is better — and more important. Their refusal to share resources with native missionaries is thus in
direct disobedience to New Testament commands about esteeming others
better than yourself, sharing and serving.

Most alert mission leaders today know better. They realize that the
fastest-growing churches in the world are spearheaded by indigenous
missionary movements. They realize that the leadership and initiative for
global evangelism must now be transferred to native leaders if the work
is to be completed.

These leaders are well aware that they are perpetuating a system that
is no longer viable. The emergence of groups such as the Third World
Mission Association, an independent indigenous mission agency, and the
increasing flow of direct support to native missionaries represent a threat
to the establishments they serve.

In fact, the very presence of visiting native missionary speakers in the
pulpits of American churches is startling new evidence of the maturing
native missions movement. The presence of indigenous missionary
leaders on Western platforms clearly reveals to the Western church that
they are no longer *the* essential link to world evangelism.

When such missionary leaders speak against native missions, too often
they appear as though trying to convince themselves and their audience
that God is not capable of completing the task of world evangelism
without *them* in control of the mission enterprise.

Painful Questions About the Future

The instinct for self-preservation is strong among the powerful advocates of conventional missions, and they are facing ever more painful
questions about the long-established practices that have sustained their
missions for decades. For example:

• Why are American young people challenged to go overseas as
missionaries even though by the time they reach the field 77 percent of
the world's population will live in countries closed to them as true
missionaries? *Right now 119 countries refuse to admit Western missionaries, and almost all of the unreached people groups are deep in the
interiors of these restricted-access countries!*[3]

• Although it is impossible to evangelize the unreached people groups
without sending native missionaries, why do many mission leaders speak

week after week in local churches without mentioning this critical situation?

• Why are funds raised, supposedly for spreading the gospel, while they are largely spent on perpetuating organizations which are involved in maintaining existing churches rather than supporting frontline missions to reach the unreached peoples?

• Why do traditional mission promoters speak only of traditional mission activities at conferences, schools and seminars while they usually ignore indigenous missions? The truth is that these events cost thousands of dollars to stage, yet they net almost nothing for the needy native workers who are most likely the ones actually doing the work of the Great Commission on the mission fields in question.

The Lausanne II conference, for example, took place as I began writing this book. It totaled $10.5 million in direct costs, plus millions more in additional costs to participants. If you count the time lost by over four thousand top leaders who attended, plus observers and staff, the actual cost probably was several times the official price tag.

If that money had been spent directly on native missionaries, it would have been enough to complete the work of world evangelism in any number of countries. This is not to say that Lausanne II was a mistake, or that we shouldn't have conferences to train and motivate workers. Only heaven knows what good is still to come from it. But the track record of these conferences in general gives us every reason to question their value. Did Lausanne I in 1974 and the dozens of its follow-up conferences make a major difference in the total number of unreached people groups in the world?

In numerous interviews conducted for this book, mission leaders could not say that there are any more Western missionaries assigned to unreached people groups now than there were in 1974. The sad truth is that after spending millions of dollars to talk to themselves in these giant conferences, Western missions are no nearer meeting the challenge of the unreached or "hidden" peoples than they were before they started.

Phil Bogosian, director of church relations in the mobilization division of the U.S. Center for World Mission, says it well: "In 1974 Lausanne I…a strong mandate was given by the Lord to His church to complete the task of world evangelization. In response thousands of global church leaders entered into 'a solemn covenant with God' stating their shame that so many had been neglected. They covenanted with God to 'pray earnestly,' 'develop a simple lifestyle,' and 'sacrifice' so that 'by all possible means and the earliest possible time' every people group could be reached.

"This has not even remotely been done — especially by the church in the West. In the course of my assignment at the U.S. Center..., I have studied church involvement in missions for about seven years. In all candor and to our continuing shame, let us admit that the world's perishing unreached peoples are very seldom mentioned or thought about in almost all churches."[4]

In a later interview Bogosian stated that he believed most mission leaders are ready and anxious to send out missionaries to unreached peoples if they could find responsiveness from denominational leadership and local churches.

We enjoy talking in general, nonspecific terms about building the "national church," but how often do you read a missionary newsletter that tells about the new congregation that was planted last week? Millions of dollars and thousands of people are engaged in studying unreached people groups, but when was the last time you read the report of a new church being formed among one of them? The simple fact, which no one wants to admit, is that our traditional mission structure is no longer doing the job. The talk is triumphant, but the facts fail to back it up.

Notes
[1]Unpublished study paper by David B. Barrett, *Global Statistics Summary* (Manila, Philippines: Lausanne II Congress on World Evangelization Statistical Task Force, July 11-20, 1989).

[2]Article by Lyn Cryderman, "Global Camp Meeting," *Christianity Today* (Wheaton, Ill.: August 18, 1989), pp. 39-41.

[3]Barrett, *Global Statistics Summary*.

[4]Article by Phil Bogosian, "Prophecy at Manila," *Mission Frontiers* (Pasadena, Calif.: U.S. Center for World Mission, August/September 1989), p. 8.

Time for
Accountability

Not too long ago I spoke at a church missions conference on the subject of this book. I encouraged the congregation to be sensitive to the changing times and to reprioritize their missions giving in light of the needs of native missionaries in the Third World. After my message a young couple asked to speak with me — I'll call them John and Mary. As they spoke I could sense a tremendous sadness in their hearts.

John had been an engineer and was bringing in a promising salary when the Lord first called him, his wife and their three children to the mission field. Convinced that the Lord was truly speaking to them, John left his secure job and went to Bible school, where he earned another degree. Then he and Mary took two years of special missionary training provided by their denomination before they were assigned to work in a South American country.

When they finally arrived at their destination, John and Mary had a great love and burden for the people they were coming to serve. As they settled into their new surroundings, they soon met the fourteen other missionaries who were working in the same region. The house that was provided for them was beautiful; in fact, it made John feel a little uncomfortable. It was one thing to be living in the most luxurious house in the entire community. It was another to realize he was enjoying better living conditions on the field than he had at home.

John soon noticed that the life-style of the local people was very different from that of the missionaries. In fact, the native evangelist who worked with him was really quite poor. His family's clothing looked worn out, and he had to work hard at a second job to provide for his family. Yet, despite their poverty, this evangelist and the other families who had come to the Lord were loving and caring in their concern for the people to whom they ministered. They had gentle servant hearts and were willing to do anything to help.

In the months that followed, however, John and Mary became aware of a troubling attitude among their fellow missionaries that went beyond the external incongruities. At first it was hard to pin down, but as time went on John discovered it pervaded every facet of the missionary life-style around them.

He saw it in the monthly missionary get-togethers, where the conversation usually ended up criticizing the local people they were supposedly serving. The missionaries had complaints to air about these people. They would give each other advice on dealing with these "locals" — whom to watch, whom to avoid and how to treat them.

John and Mary became burdened about this situation, but they really didn't know what to do except pray. Then one day something happened that demanded action.

They had gone to a fellow missionary's house for a visit. While the two couples were talking, a knock was heard at the door. The missionary's wife answered it to find one of the senior native pastors. She invited him into the living room with the other three missionaries. He stayed only a few minutes to discuss a matter with them, and then he left.

As soon as he left, the missionary's wife immediately brought out a can of Lysol and sprayed it on the chair where the native pastor had sat. As she wiped, she fussed, "They know they are not supposed to sit in these chairs. We have chairs outside on the porch where they can sit if they want to talk!" Then she told John and Mary how to keep the natives at a distance. "Otherwise," she said, "they will have no respect."

This was more than enough for John and Mary. After going home and discussing it further, they sent a letter to their mission board. "If we are allowed to live on the standard of the local people we minister to and maintain their life-style, only then do we feel we can continue on the field," John wrote.

Word soon got back to the field of John and Mary's letter. The primary reaction of the missionaries to the couple's decision was shock. But within a year's time they had completely ostracized John and Mary and their family. The mission board's response was simple: "Come home." So they left the mission field and the people they had come to minister to because they were not allowed to live among them.

When John and Mary finished their story, they were both weeping. "What you said tonight was so true," they said. "If only you would share what you said tonight with every church and every mission organization in this country!"

Sending churches are being led to believe that traditional missions are growing and effective. Part of the reformation we need in missions includes stricter measures for accountability than have ever been demanded before. We desperately need to have honest reporting from the mission field. And we need to understand how keenly some truly devoted missionaries regret seeing the shabby treatment of worthy native missionaries.

No objective agency polices overseas missions. The only reports most Western supporters receive are the self-serving ones generated by the mission leaders for fund-raising purposes.

Today's generation of Western missionaries is too often like an army camped on the banks of a river. Every day they talk about crossing to the other side. Their commander has ordered them to cross. They have many methods available — building a bridge, ferrying over or even swimming. Now suppose these soldiers put on river-crossing displays and conduct river-crossing conferences year after year — but never cross the river. Wouldn't you have every right to think there was something seriously wrong? Yet this is exactly the current status of Western missions.

Why has the Western church suspended logical thinking and action in this one area, choosing to go according to the ways of this world rather than Scripture? Why do we hold back and cling to our old ways?

The "unspoken topics" no one wants to talk about fall into five basic categories: (1) our prejudice against native missionaries, (2) our spiritual powerlessness, (3) our missionary life-styles, (4) our stewardship of funds and (5) our lack of authenticity in staff appointments. These are the five big no-no subjects in missions today. Since we can't and won't talk about them, our healing has been postponed again and again!

The Mission World's Best-kept Secret

Why can't we acknowledge the contribution of indigenous groups to modern missions? In my first book, *The Coming Revolution in World Missions,* I called them "God's third wave." Natives are now completing what colonial missions began.

The native missionary movement is already the cornerstone of world evangelism today, but you'd never know it from missions propaganda in the West. European and American Christians have no idea of the importance of indigenous missions because reports in the Western media chronically ignore the presence of native missionaries.

As I was writing this chapter, the spring 1989 edition of the ACMC newsletter came across my desk. The Association of Church Missions Committees is one of the most powerful mission groups in the United States, with eight hundred member churches.

On the front page some interesting statistics appeared, supplied by scholars at the Midwest Center for World Mission, one of the many regional centers inspired by the U.S. Center for World Mission in Pasadena, California. The editor reported the Midwest center relied on MARC and Global Mapping for their information — two very fine research organizations considered authoritative by mission scholars in the United States.

The chart listed twenty-six countries that are top priority for North American "tentmaking missionaries." To build its case, the chart purports to reveal how many "missionaries" and "churches" are in each country.

The two most unreached countries were China and India, with a total of 5,025 unreached people groups. According to the chart, China has only 26 missionaries, and India 834 — all from the United States and Britain. India has only 2,198 churches, and China's number of churches is listed as "not available." Because the Midwest center does not recognize the contribution of native missions and indigenous churches not controlled by Anglo-American mission boards, it has misinformed the ACMC membership about the true nature of the task before us in China and India.[1]

Here are a few facts not mentioned:

(1) The 860 North American missionaries reported in these countries are actually social workers and technical-support people, not missionaries involved in evangelism or church planting. Virtually the only evangelism and church planting being done in China and India are being done by native missions! The combined efforts of much-publicized tourists, tentmakers and Bible smugglers to China result in such an insignificant number of converts or church start-ups that no one keeps a record.

(2) In India I conservatively estimate that there are now at least 10,000 native missionaries engaged in full-time, New Testament witness. China probably has at least the same amount or more. The report ignores these numbers.

(3) Nobody really knows how many churches there are in India, but the number is probably a lot closer to 200,000 than it is to the mere 2,198 listed. There are probably that many Bible-believing churches in the tiny state of Nagaland alone. Based on an estimate of 70 million Christians in China, meeting in house churches averaging 30 members each, there would have to be about two million churches in China.

Even Bishop H.K. Ting of the official Three Self church movement admits that there are now two Protestant churches reopening in China every three days — and, of course, that doesn't even count the unofficial house churches![2]

Why didn't ACMC and the Midwest center report on the number of indigenous churches and missions on these two fields now closed to American missionaries? When we asked the editor the reason for the obvious distortion, he said he expects all his readers to take statistics like these with "a grain of salt," knowing that they aren't accurate!

"Why print them then?" we asked.

The reason, he said, was to give the compilers of the chart a chance to show the need for tentmakers to go from the United States — and the native church and mission figures don't contribute to making the point.

"Does that mean," we asked, "that it is all right to lie to make a point?"

"No," he replied, "but I see our newsletter as a forum for thought, and the Midwest center was trying to build a case for tentmakers."

That such distortions occur when Western mission boards report only their North American missionary activity is regrettable. What is tragic is that millions of souls for whom Christ died may remain unreached because funds are withheld from the thousands of native missionaries eager to be about their Lord's business.

This is only one example of the way native missionaries are misrepresented in the West. Missions magazines and other communications consistently distort the actual situation on the field in many other ways.

First, they invariably under-report the actual number of native missionaries on a field. This is done by ignoring native missionaries not affiliated with their association or denomination or meeting other Western-based criteria.

Second, they describe native missionaries in terms that make them appear unqualified or less than qualified in comparison to the white missionaries.

Third, through photographs and art, they paint a picture of a substandard ministry being carried on by indigenous missionaries.

Yet the most destructive reporting of all is "nonreporting" — simply choosing to cover overseas situations through Western eyes, ignoring the presence and contribution of indigenous missions. This is an editorial policy unconsciously applied to missions reporting by nearly all Christian media in the West, even those which are not particularly missions-oriented. Even the most professional, careful journalists slip into stereotypes when writing mission stories.

Not only are selective reporting and nonreporting a tragic sign of this prejudice against native missionaries, but even more blatant is the attitude of the missionary on the field against his national co-worker.

I believe the problem John and Mary struggled with goes beyond prejudice. There is a much stronger word to describe the sinful attitude that is still prevalent in the hearts of many colonial-era missionaries and mission leaders. We need to recognize this underlying mind-set and call it by its true name — racism.

During my years of ministry in Asia, I've traveled through many Third World countries where some Western missionaries still live in established centers. It is unfortunate that even in this modern age some missionaries still treat the most educated, enlightened, godly, capable indigenous leaders as servants or less than equal — simply because the color of their skin and their culture are different.

Notes

[1] Article by Mike Pollard, "Jumping on the Bandwagon," *ACMC Newsletter* (Wheaton, Ill.: ACMC, Spring 1989), p. 1.

[2] Article, unsigned, "China Opens Wider Door for Nora," *China Today Newspaper* (San Jose, Calif.: Nora Lam Chinese Ministries International, Spring 1990), p.1.

Our Spiritual
Powerlessness

As Western missions have grown increasingly effete, a strange phenomenon has occurred: *the social sciences appear to have altered mission strategy.* Western missionaries have introduced education and communication theory as a complement to preaching the gospel.

This is understandable. The lure of human knowledge and wisdom is powerful. Many missionaries today attempt to accommodate the gospel to the religion and philosophy of the culture when they try intellectually to defeat animism, Buddhism, Islam or Hinduism.

Paul's experience with education and religious philosophy suggests another approach in 1 Corinthians 2:1-2: "And I, brethren, when I came to you, came not with excellency of speech or of wisdom, declaring unto you the testimony of God. For I determined not to know any thing among you, save Jesus Christ, and him crucified."

In my early years as a street-preaching evangelist in North India, I had to learn this lesson the hard way. I read everything I could to defeat Hindu and Muslim philosophy — including the *Bhagavad-Gita, Rama-*

yana, Koran and other non-Christian scriptures.

The better my apologetics skills became, the more I relied on my logic and knowledge. Time and again, I found myself winning arguments — but not converts. Early one morning in my quiet time I read Hebrews 4:12: "For the word of God is quick, and powerful, and sharper than any twoedged sword, piercing even to the dividing asunder of soul and spirit, and of the joints and marrow, and is a discerner of the thoughts and intents of the heart."

That morning, as I climbed onto the tailgate of our gospel van to preach, I determined that I would preach "as a blind man to voiceless people." At that moment I threw out my communication theory. I laid aside my sophistry, anti-Hindu arguments, and knowledge of local religious philosophy and culture. Instead, I expounded the simple gospel to my Hindu audience. I talked about sin, salvation, faith and repentance.

To my surprise, a Hindu teenager came forward, weeping in repentance to accept Jesus Christ — the living God whom he had never heard of before that sermon.

The lesson was heaven-sent: We must not rely on our knowledge and education to win the nations to Christ. As I led the youth to Christ, it was obvious to me that if I had argued against his religious prejudice that morning, he never would have come to find the Savior.

Education is not wrong in itself. The desire to understand and communicate with heathen cultures is often sincere and well-intentioned, but it short-circuits the power of the gospel.

Efforts to communicate to the natural mind of man do not bring radical conversion. The gospel goes straight to the heart of man. It converts the spirit, not the head.

So much of modern missions theory relies on man-made principles, including what is passing itself off today as church-growth and people-movement strategy. Many of these sociology-based notions rely on exploiting ungodly social sins such as the Hindu caste system, racial segregation and economic classes.

Along with applied psychology, many of these principles are the same ones used as a basis for secular mass-marketing technology in the West. As a result the power of the Holy Spirit is frequently ignored.

After missiologists have presented their doctoral theses and shown their overhead transparencies, mission committees should ask some of these questions before they send a check:

• Where in the Bible is this approach to missions taught? What especially did Jesus and Paul say about your particular theory of church growth?

• On which fields have you successfully implemented the strategy or theory being proposed?

• Is there any historical precedent for using this method? If so, was the methodology central to what happened or incidental to a larger movement of the Holy Spirit? What role did simple preaching by native missionary evangelists and pastors play in the church-growth movement used as an example?

• Will the implementation of this theory cause the indigenous church to be dependent on direction and leadership by foreign missionaries, special funding, equipment and supplies unavailable on the local economy, or other materials that must be imported from the West?

Our Missionary Life-styles

My good friend David Mains, radio host of "The Chapel of the Air," presented an unforgettable challenge to attendees at the National Religious Broadcasters' annual convention in Washington, D.C. He based his message on the best-selling book *The Accidental Tourist* by Anne Tyler.

David began his talk by passing out an ugly, wrought-iron nail to everyone in the audience. At first the mysterious nail was not explained.

The story line in *The Accidental Tourist* revolves around a jaded writer named Macon who turns out travel guides for American business people going overseas. Anne Tyler describes Macon and his work this way: "He covered only the cities in these guides, for people taking business trips flew into cities and out again and didn't see the countryside at all. They didn't see the cities for that matter. Their concern was how to pretend they had never left home."[1]

In this case David applied the message of *The Accidental Tourist* to the convention delegates. He challenged them to attend the NRB convention as they imagined Jesus would have attended. He gave four rules for this, which also apply perfectly to missionary work:

(1) Don't be thinking constantly about yourself and your agenda.

(2) Show genuine interest in what others are doing, viewing them as better than yourself.

(3) Make your bottom line the advancement of the common cause.

(4) Pray daily that you and your fellow workers will be drawn together in Christ's love.

Then the nail began to make sense. No believer can impact people effectively until he, like Christ, is willing to open his palm and receive the nail. We have to die to ourselves in order to bring life to the lost. David challenged the delegates to carry that nail throughout the convention as a reminder to work at being Christlike.

The same applies to our missionary outreach. How I wish every missionary would carry a nail around with him at all times! Foreign missionaries need to be reminded that they will be effective only to the degree that they are willing to surrender their own culture and adopt that of the people to be reached.

The greatest cultural barrier between Western missionaries and the local population is still their alien, extravagant life-styles. A visit to the average missionary home is the ultimate turn-off for the natives on most mission fields — especially in Hindu, Muslim or Buddhist cultures.

A missionary simply cannot set a Christlike example and make disciples if he is trying to live with one foot in each culture. Native Christians must be able to see you cope with the same struggles they do, in the same way, in order to see the power of the living God at work in their culture.

If they see you minister in their culture and then go home to your family and retreat in your own culture, it sets up obstacles the nationals cannot overlook. In light of the barriers which alien, high standards of living tend to raise, we need to ask some critical life-style questions of every Western missionary we support. For example:

• Why is it necessary to maintain Western-style homes, own cars and import foreign foods on the mission field? Can't missionaries take local buses and live in homes as natives do? Why won't they adjust to the local cuisine?

• Why is it necessary to take vacation-furloughs to the homeland, use separate medical facilities and begin missionary ministry in special language schools and institutional environments which separate the missionary psychologically from the local people?

• Why is it necessary to maintain a circle of foreign friends, attend English-language worship services and live segregated lives from the rest of the population?

• Why are cooks, drivers, maids and other servants so often a part of missionary life-styles in the Third World?

• Why wear imported clothes and shoes, use imported appliances and own other luxury goods that are not indigenous to the culture? Why must missionary homes be air-conditioned or heated when those of the average natives are not?

• Why build or use compounds, church halls and institutions that have a foreign appearance and are furnished in a way that creates culture-shock for native visitors?

• Why are liturgy, music and worship styles on the mission field similar to those in the homeland of the missionary? Why are Christian religious art and even the musical instruments of worship imported from the West?

Are these questions about superficial matters? Perhaps in a few cases, but every missionary needs to pray through these questions in the light of his or her particular assignment. In most cases it is arrogance that separates them from the unreached people they came to serve and win to Christ. The reason traditional Western missionaries prefer to live as foreigners often is their dislike for the ways of those among whom they work, or their unwillingness to give up Western comforts.

Am I saying I believe effective missionaries must "go native" and sacrifice their culture and way of life to reach the lost? Absolutely yes.

Do I think it is ever possible to lose your identity in the culture? Probably not in most cases — but even if it isn't possible, I think every missionary must try. Adopting local customs, dress, food and language may seem merely symbolic, but it is the first and essential step in identifying with the local people.

Ultimately, only to the degree that the missionary neutralizes his own alien cultural barriers will he successfully plant indigenous churches. This is one reason why Jesus chose to be born a Jew and be raised in a Jewish home. How could He ever fully identify with the Jews and become their Savior if He didn't forsake His heavenly kingdom, language and life-style to become one with mankind and the Jews?

What about adopting a bicultural life-style? There may be a few situations on university campuses, in large urban centers, in "base-towns" around foreign military bases or ministries to servicemen or other specialists where a so-called bicultural ministry might work. But in most cases the use of this term is merely semantics — an excuse Western missionaries use to keep double standards. What is a bicultural person in any real indigenous culture? Is it not just another word for being a foreigner?

The real unreached people groups are almost always rural, tight-knit, closed cultures. Successful disciple making and church planting require maximum identification with the local people and death to the culture of the incoming missionary.

If missionaries are not willing to try at least to forsake their culture and live like the people they reach, how can they expect to be able to transfer spiritual life to their disciples?

Foreign missionaries will give a hundred reasons why they can't try to identify with the people. Many of these reasons are ones involving children, family and government restrictions. However, in the end they start to sound like better reasons for not going overseas than for attempting to live a life in the cultural schizophrenia imposed by colonial-style missions practice.

Every missionary must be willing to answer some painful questions:

How long have you been on the field, and how many disciples have you made?

How many churches have you planted?

What spiritual impact have you made on the people among whom you minister?

If the answers are unacceptable, part of the reason is probably that he or she can't, or won't, pay the price to sacrifice the comfort, culture, freedom, position, power, riches and rights of being a foreigner in Third World society.

If you can't give up your culture, consider whether God has called you to "go" or to be a "sender." The problem, frankly, with so many of us is our unwillingness to face the fact that Jesus called us all to be servants, not masters.

I cringe when I hear Western leaders talk of "using the nationals." We're not to *use* anyone in the kingdom. An authentic, New Testament missionary must give up the idea that he is superior and has the right to use anyone else.

Most often the personal life-styles we choose for ourselves and our families reflect the heart of our management and ministry styles more than anything else we do. Westerners on the mission field instinctively choose a life-style they feel comfortable with, that of a detached overseer.

Instead, we need missionaries who are forever feeling those nails in the palms of their hands, surrendering their ways to His ways — like Paul, becoming all things to all men in order that they might win some.

Few foreign missionaries from the West even begin to demonstrate the art of living as Jesus did, and their sending churches do little to prepare them for this kind of commitment. Because of this, the cause of Christ would be better served without them. Western Christianity and society are not presently producing many Christians of this caliber — the kind of person willing to live that life-style of sacrifice and selflessness required on the mission fields of the Third World.

Notes

[1]Article by David Mains, "Working at Being Christlike," *Reveille Magazine* (Wheaton, Ill.: The Chapel of the Air, June 1989), p. 6.

---------------- 14 ----------------

Our Stewardship
of Funds

A missionary who spent years in Sri Lanka and India, where he successfully discipled a number of native missionary workers, now invests his life in raising sponsorships for them in the United States and Canada. He is convinced this is the best stewardship of his time and talents, even though he was more effective on the field than most foreigners.

"Right now," says Terry Jones, "we know beyond a shadow of a doubt that we're having a more effective impact on Asia than we did when we were there. I believe that because of the hundreds of sponsors I've helped to raise up for native missionaries here, I have multiplied my missionary effectiveness thousands of times."

George Otis Jr. is among the small band of thoughtful missions leaders who are wondering out loud if we can still afford to keep sending traditional missionaries overseas.

In 1989 he wrote, "The cost of maintaining a missionary family in Kenya or Zambia today runs in the vicinity of $45,000. Placing a missionary family in Japan, however, is an even greater fiscal adventure.

First-year expenses there can easily top $100,000, with subsequent maintenance costs in the neighborhood of $55,000 to $65,000 (annually). In Brazil, the nation with the greatest number of North American missionaries, hyperinflation (currently running at an annual rate of 1,000 percent) threatens to push support costs through the roof. On balance, the cost of supporting a conventional American missionary abroad has risen 75 percent over the last five years."[1]

Compared to traditional missionaries, native missionaries are a bargain indeed. In Japan, where the per capita annual income was $10,100 in 1987,[2] Japanese leaders say the typical cost of supporting a native missionary is only $24,000 per year. This is 48 percent of what it takes to maintain a foreign missionary ($49,896).[3]

In economically volatile Brazil, the per capita annual income was $1,890 by one mission's calculations.[4] It costs only about $3,700 a year to support a Brazilian native missionary. This is 17 percent of one mission's average ($21,456), 11 percent of another mission's staffer ($31,392) and 8 percent of a third ($41,997).[5]

In Asia, more than anywhere else, the difference is amazing. In China the per capita annual income is only $290, in Vietnam $600, in India $260.[6] It is still possible to support native missionaries working in village evangelistic bands for as little as $30 to $90 monthly. In cities and other situations, of course, the cost can multiply, but the average native missionary supported by Gospel for Asia is still living on $30 to $120 a month.

It is not unusual right now for Western missionaries living almost anywhere in Asia to have to raise $36,000 to $50,000 annually, particularly in urbanized areas in Thailand and the Philippines.

So, once again, supporting a Western missionary to poor Asian nations becomes an awesome investment, especially when you consider the longer period of training required for foreigners.

John Maxwell, pastor of Skyline Wesleyan, the largest Wesleyan church in the world, says we need to ask ourselves this bottom-line question: What is the return on investment for all the missions money that we give every year?

To illustrate his point Maxwell places traditional missions and the indigenous missions movement side by side:

"Let's look at a typical profile of a [single] missionary educated in the United States: four years of college, $60,000; two years of seminary,

$40,000; one year of raising support, $20,000; two years of language school, $50,000...and one year net work at $20,000.

"...After eleven years of training and $210,000 investment, you have sent one missionary to serve one year.

"Let's look at a similar scenario in the Philippines....Here is how it breaks down: two years of Bible school, $2,000. After two years of training at the cost of $2,000 you now have a missionary on the field evangelizing [for the cost of about $1,000 per year in support]."

Maxwell carries this even further, adding, "You can have one American missionary on the field for fifteen years, costing the church $585,000 — over half a million dollars — or a Filipino missionary, trained and on the field for fifteen years at a cost to the church of $17,000.

"For the same amount of money that it takes to train and supply one American missionary to the Philippines, we could support thirty-five national missionaries. *Look at the difference.*"[7]

Can missions still afford this long, costly investment, especially when it is no longer necessary on most mission fields? Native missionaries can routinely be organizing their first church in six months to two years of arriving at their assignment. Recruiting time for native missionaries is usually only weeks or months since most native missionaries are already involved in Christian service and need only be moved to an area which is unevangelized. Even when they have to learn a new language, it is frequently quite similar to their own. Thought patterns, food and dress can be readily adapted by a culturally near native missionary. All this results in reduced costs.

Mission leaders and sending churches must start asking the tough questions about their financial stewardship. For example:

• How much did it cost to present the gospel to each hearer last year as a mission overall, as a field, as an individual missionary?

• How much would it have cost to support a native missionary to do the same evangelistic work? Would it be more efficient and effective for us to support native missionaries?

• How much was the average cost to start up a new church last year as a mission overall, as a field, as an individual missionary?

• How much would it have cost to support a native missionary to do the same church-planting work?

• In terms of pure proclamation, how much would it cost per thousand to blanket an unreached people group with gospel radio, literature,

newspaper, poster and tract evangelism?
   • What would it cost to assist native workers with other simple tools such as Bibles, cassettes, flip charts and audio-visuals?
   • In your mission program, how are both foreign and native missionaries accountable for the funds entrusted to them? Are results measured in terms of return on investment, or does financial accountability end with only a financial audit in the U.S. offices?
   • What about overhead costs on the field and in the United States? How much of each donation is used for direct ministry and how much for overhead?
   • What about conference attendance, missionary consultations and other strategy sessions? How does your mission program attach numbers and measure results from these meetings in terms of converts, new churches planted and missions launched to unreached people groups? Are we getting benefit out of these meetings equal to their cost?
   • As we look toward completing the missionary task, how much is it going to cost to complete a church start-up in each of the twelve thousand unreached people groups still without a witness? How much is it going to cost using Western personnel and methods? How much is it going to cost using indigenous personnel and methods?
   Measuring the results of missionary investment by ratios and forcing ourselves to answer the hard financial questions is a painful process — especially for missionary bureaucrats who have never really made themselves accountable before.
   If we view the self-evaluation process as an adventure rather than a way to judge one another and fix blame, it can be wonderfully constructive and liberating. However, as we go through the evaluation process, we must never forget that not all fields are alike. In fact, not all situations are alike, even in the same country. Sometimes we are sowing seed spiritually and breaking up fallow ground. Sometimes we are blessed to be in harvest time.
   Naturally it is going to cost far more in terms of finances and people to penetrate resistant unreached people groups than the more open ones. Costs of living in cities are more expensive than in rural areas, but you can often reach more people faster in cities. These and many other factors need to be considered prayerfully when we evaluate missionary finances.
   But just because it is sometimes difficult to be a good steward doesn't mean missions or missionaries should be left unaccountable!

Even though some ministries are by definition more expensive than others, we will be truly foolish if we continue to finance missions without counting the costs and finding ways to do the work more effectively and efficiently.

A recent article in the *Evangelical Missions Quarterly* titled "Confessions of a Sender" addresses the need for an open line of communication and accountability between "goers" and "senders": "I believe that stewardship is the issue. Stewardship on my part demands that I pay attention to how the funds that I give are spent...when missionaries are not serving responsibly..., should not their senders know about this? We are not a partnership until we do."[8]

Appointing Authentic Missionaries

I'll never forget the fascinating talk I once had with a so-called village development missionary in Nepal. This man had been in the country for twenty-two years. We talked about his work and the gospel, and I learned that during that time he had not won a single soul to Christ, let alone planted a church.

Incredulous, I questioned him about the nature of his work. He had learned the language and obviously had a lot of contact with local people of all kinds since he was digging tube wells. His work took him out to remote villages, and it was hard to imagine that the subject of his faith could be avoided.

Indeed, it was hard to believe he wouldn't have some kind of opportunity to witness and that his life wouldn't attract somebody to Christ. But he was adamant. He truly believed with all his heart that God had called him to dig wells and that this was his ministry.

He didn't preach or witness because he honestly didn't believe that was part of his job description. Although I'm sure the directors of his mission in New York City probably felt he was doing a great job, I couldn't help but wonder what the folks in his church back home would think if they could hear his explanation. I dare say a good many of them gave to their mission because they assumed this man would be extending the kingdom of God — even if he was digging wells as a vocation.

Although this well-digging missionary had his theological rationalization down pat, I'm certain his work would not be considered authentic missionary ministry by most lay people in the denomination that sent him out.

Does that mean we don't need social workers, pastors and support people? Of course not. There is a legitimate need for these people in many local church situations on the field. But in most cases they should rightfully be getting their support from the local congregations on the field — not from mission funds. And certainly not while we still have nearly three billion people without a Christian witness.

While I was writing this chapter, a California congregation invited me to present the challenge for native missionaries. When the pastor gave the final challenge to his people on the last night, 160 people pledged to support a full-time native missionary. The congregation was already supporting 40, so now they fully support 200 native missionaries. And these missionaries are working in pioneer situations on the front lines of the gospel.

The cost for sending out 200 of these native missionaries is $216,000 a year. If they were contributing to traditional American missionaries with that same money, how many could they send? It will come as a shock to you: only three missionaries to Japan; or seven to eight missionaries to the Philippines; or ten to eleven missionaries to rural Third World countries.

The decision is obvious. Unless there is some compelling reason, it makes overwhelming sense to support native missionaries rather than foreign missionaries.

What Needs to Be Done?

Plainly, we must talk openly about this serious problem and study the alternatives. We would do so in a minute if we treated missions as seriously as we do our business transactions.

How much easier it would have been for me to write this book without this chapter. It is seldom pleasant to speak the truth in love — but the Bible commands us to do so. Peter insists that "judgment must begin at the house of God" (1 Pet. 4:17), and so we need to recognize this foolishness as the sin it is and forsake it.

At times it seems as if God says to us, "My child, it is time for a radical change. Put your house in order." I have had to do this in my own life, and I believe God is now calling on Western church leaders to take this kind of action concerning our current missions programs. We must be honest with ourselves and make changes. The only way we as the body of Christ can begin walking in the light is by opening up and admitting our weaknesses.

The beautiful thing is, when we confess our sins and turn the control back over to Him, the Holy Spirit rushes in with cleansing and power. What wonderful things the Lord will do in our lives if we only surrender our "hidden corners" to His light of truth.

Homer Firestone and David Miller, missionaries to Bolivia, agree: "Self-examination, although painful, can be tremendously beneficial. Repentance is a great way to make new beginnings. Healing and reconciliation are central themes of the gospel. Everyone in the missions enterprise — board members, administrators, missionaries, and church leaders — ought to include these elements in their working agendas."[9]

Notes

[1]Article by George Otis Jr. "We Could Learn Some Lessons From the Business World," *ACMC Newsletter* (Wheaton, Ill.: ACMC, Spring 1989), pp. 6-7.

[2]Patrick Johnstone, *Operation World — Fourth Edition* (Waynesboro, Ga.: Send the Light/WEC Publications, 1987), p. 258.

[3]Comparative statistics in these paragraphs contrast telephone spot checks with mission field sources at the time of writing, George Otis's 1989 research on salary figures, and Operation World 1987 references. Despite the obvious time gaps, they still accurately portray the relative disparity in salary costs.

[4]Johnstone, *Operation World*, p. 112.

[5]See footnote 3.

[6]Johnstone, *Operation World*, pp. 137, 215, 446.

[7]Sermon by John Maxwell at Skyline Wesleyan Church, May 6, 1990.

[8]Anonymous article, "Confessions of a Sender," *Evangelical Missions Quarterly* (Wheaton, Ill.: Evangelical Missions Information Service, October 1990), pp. 445-446.

[9]Article by Homer L. Firestone and David Miller, "Mission Boards: The Self-Critical Alternative," *Evangelical Missions Quarterly* (Wheaton, Ill.: Evangelical Missions Information Service, October 1990), p. 414.

Book II

Rewards of Sponsoring
Native Missionaries

The tiny congregation of the Church of the Blue Ridge near Waynesboro, Virginia, numbers only thirty adults. But one thing they do possess is a missionary vision — and their board of elders is serious about frontline evangelism. For some time they have wanted to make a significant impact in evangelizing an unreached people group.

So in the spring of 1989 the elders contacted one of the handful of American mission societies which specialize in helping indigenous missions. "Could our church help sponsor the evangelization of one of the twelve thousand unreached people groups still without an established Christian witness?" they asked.

Within minutes a missions executive was checking his files of indigenous missionary groups in the Philippines. Using his Unreached Peoples Data Base from Global Mapping International in Pasadena, California, he matched the church with a gospel team. This team had targeted the unreached Waray Waray tribe in Leyte, Philippines, for their next evangelistic thrust.

He discovered that a nearby indigenous mission board would be able to send a team of three Filipino missionaries to the Waray Waray people for only $550 a month. This would cover their transportation, housing, support, government-required taxes and supplies.

The elders of the tiny church were astonished at the huge impact their tiny missions budget could have overseas. By investing their limited resources in native missionaries, they could help eliminate one of the last of the twelve thousand unreached people groups still remaining on the planet.

In June the elders presented their vision to the whole congregation using maps and slides from the Philippines. Looking up the Waray Waray people in the *Ethnologue* from Wycliffe Bible Translators, one of the elders discovered a lot about this hostile, difficult-to-reach people.

There were two million in the northern and eastern parts of Leyte — making them one of the largest unreached people groups in the world. Except for nominal Roman Catholics and some cults, no Christian group had yet established a viable work among them — this in spite of the fact that revival and spectacular church growth continue in many other parts of the Philippines.

That Sunday morning the congregation prayed and pledged to send the nearby indigenous gospel team to help reach the Waray Waray. To recruit, train and send three American families would have taken years. Tragically, the Blue Ridge church wouldn't have been able to afford such support since the annual cost would have been at least $84,360 for three American missionaries.

The High Cost of Foreign Personnel

According to a study conducted by a conservative mission board in the Philippines, each American couple would have needed an annual budget of $2,400 for language training, $720 for support-raising "prayer letters," $1,200 for contingencies, $2,100 for insurance and social security, and $1,500 for furlough fund. None of this is needed by the indigenous native missionaries.

The other comparisons are equally amazing. The American couple would need $6,000 for field work expenses; the Filipinos only $132. Miscellaneous costs for the Americans, $1,200; for the Filipinos, $67. A car for the Americans, $3,000 annually amortized over five years — for the Filipinos, only $67 for jeepney fares.

Housing costs for the American couple, $4,800; for the Filipinos, $267. Personal family needs for the Americans were $7,200 as opposed to $667 for the Filipino missionaries.[1]

This study is based on the average costs of supporting an American missionary family in the Philippines. It might vary for work among the Waray Waray somewhat, but the cost differential is amazing no matter where you make the comparison. Many missionary couples in Manila and remote assignments in the Philippines are raising even more; it is not unusual to see budgets ranging from $40,000 to $50,000 now.

What a challenge it will be for this little group of Americans to pray for their Filipino witness band and share in this pioneer work among one of the world's most lost and forgotten peoples.

Acts 1:8 Is for Every Church

Yet isn't this a direct fulfillment of the promise the Lord Jesus gave the church as recorded in Acts 1:8? "And ye shall be witnesses unto me both in Jerusalem, and in all Judaea, and in Samaria, and unto the uttermost part of the earth." This local church is enjoying the excitement of seeing that prophecy fulfilled through their global and local outreach.

What an awesome and comprehensive command the Great Commission is — not only sending us out to cover the geography of the world, but to be part of seeing the gospel supernaturally cross barriers of culture as well. Obviously, in the Great Commission, the Lord Jesus intended us to miss no one with the gospel.

The implications of fulfilling such a worldwide commission are staggering. How could Christ have actually expected us to be involved simultaneously in multicultural ministries locally and to the uttermost part of the earth?

That means translating the gospel into 5,500 major world languages with thousands of additional variations of these languages, including 30,000 dialects. It means accommodating it to 11,500 major ethnolinguistic groups further subdivided into 60,000 mini-cultures or tribes, and even further subdivided into 250,000 clans — what anthropologists call culture complexes.

It means identifying with five major world races further divided into about 70 mini-races. And it means crossing 250 national and political frontiers that have taken millenniums to construct.

And, in today's world, we also now have 307 mega-cities that are becoming almost cultures unto themselves.[2] Urban evangelism, because it addresses so many cultures and needs simultaneously, is one of the greatest challenges facing the church today.

Yet it is obvious that Christ literally meant for us to reach out to this whole world — apparently in something almost like concentric circles according to the Acts 1:8 rendering of the Great Commission.

Does that command mean that everyone in the body of Christ must literally and personally be responsible to go into the whole world? Does it mean each local church must literally send members from its own congregation to the whole world? Of course not. There is no other logical way to fulfill this assignment but to help support many different missions which at the same time will reach not only our own cities, states and nations, but the rest of the world as well.

Yet today many people believe the Great Commission means they should go into all the world and make clones of themselves. Sometimes these clones bear labels like Anglican, Baptist, Catholic, evangelical or Pentecostal. At other times the labels are related to special ministries, outreaches, issues, causes and vocations too numerous to name.

So many North American denominations, missions and parachurch organizations have come to be obsessed with their own private interpretations of Acts 1:8. No other scripture is so often interpreted in an unhealthy way as some form of exclusive, private mandate. That's why we find many missions constantly reinventing the wheel, embarking on overlapping projects and putting their "brand name" on redundant campaigns and church-building programs.

Not a Personal, But a Corporate Mandate

The Great Commission is not given to one individual, to one local church or even to one race or denomination or nation. However, I sense that many in the church in North America cling to a false belief that they are the only ones who can reach the world for Christ. This kind of thinking reflects a paternalistic attitude in its basest form.

Rudy Barlaan, a linguist and lecturer with Wycliffe Bible Translators and a native Filipino, describes some signs of a paternalistic mind-set: (1) *a feeling of indispensability* — "they can't do it without us"; (2) *an attitude of excessive pity* — "those poor people need our help"; (3) *an attitude of overprotection* — "they can't make decisions for them-selves"; (4) *an excessive feeling of responsibility* — "we have to meet their needs"; and (5) *a feeling of sovereignty* — "we're in control."[3]

The late Charles Troutman, former general director of InterVarsity Christian Fellowship, warned, "Paternalism is not just a harmless attitude but a despicable curse. It is a denial of the integrity of the individual as a responsible person. It denies that the Holy Spirit is capable of transforming and developing anyone.

"Paternalism robs us of the confidence that God can do what we cannot, and gives us built-in arrogance that we cannot hide."[4]

But Western missions are slow to give up this paternalism. So many organizations remain rooted in doctrinal pride and superior attitudes. And because of this most of the grand designs that come from the Western church are either stillborn or headed for an early grave. Missions that attempt to impose alien organizations, programs or talents are doomed. Oh, that we would pray as David did, "Keep back thy servant also from presumptuous sins" (Ps. 19:13).

Meanwhile, the mission fields of the world are still waiting for those truly called of God — those who will give up their efforts to impress others and abandon their own agendas, plans and pet doctrines.

Where are the meek who will joyfully demonstrate that they are indeed slaves of Christ? Where are those who will take up the towel as Jesus did and become servants to His servants? That kind of missionary leader is irresistible — though you seldom see him at the podium or covered by the media. He is too busy, out doing the work.

The Hidden Missionaries

Such missionary leaders already exist on most of the world's mission fields. Very few of them have ever slept in a five-star hotel. Often, even though they have a burden for the lost and unreached, they are faithfully serving the Lord in existing churches as lay leaders. Few of them are ordained by men. They usually lack degrees from Western seminaries or Bible schools — yet they are compelled by the love of God to witness and gather converts into the church. They usually are known only by their fruits.

They don't wear the robes and collars of clergy. They have no special rank or status. Though frequently considered the offscouring of the earth, these "barefoot missionaries" are often the *best-qualified* and *most gifted* for the work.

These are the hidden missionaries — ready to be called, commissioned and sent forth to carry the gospel to the unreached villages, peoples and nations. On almost every mission field, thousands of dedicated servants wait only to be identified and sent into the harvest field.

Does this mean we should put a premium on sending out ignorant and uneducated missionaries? No, education is important. But not the kind so many Western missionaries and churches refer to when they glibly declare, "We must train the nationals."

The training they receive will be based in their home countries — thousands of small Bible schools found in the far-flung corners of their native lands. These local training centers educate thirty to fifty students at a time, in their mother tongue, with hands-on experience and solid Bible teaching. After two to three years of intensive study and labor, they are deeply rooted in God's Word, well-equipped by godly leaders and ready to go into the unreached areas.

Does this mean we should put a premium on recruiting the simple and unsophisticated?

No, on the contrary, the best missionaries are those who are well aware of worldly planning methods — yet have chosen to renounce human wisdom and rely on God for divine wisdom. They are not stupid but have chosen to trust God rather than man for their success. But because they haven't yet learned Madison Avenue marketing and fund-raising techniques, they are invisible to the West and its missionary machinery. So they go unsupported and unreported.

No Shortage After All

The best news for world evangelism is this: *They are already there!* While mission leaders in the West are wringing their hands at the lack of new missionaries from traditional Western sources, thousands of spiritually qualified missionary candidates are waiting on the field to be sent to the hidden peoples.

There is no lack or shortage of missionaries in our world today. All the staff needed to complete the harvest is already out there — often gleaning in a nearby field because they don't have the means to get to the untouched harvest. Today an almost unlimited source of missionary labor waits to be commissioned and sent into the ripened fields.

We will never finish world evangelization in our generation until we reverse our thinking. We must stop viewing the missionary problem as, How can we get more white missionaries from here to go there? Instead we must adopt a field perspective. *We must discover the power of sending the nearest native missionary.* We'll know the task has reached completion stages when the primary talk of sending churches is not about transferring missionaries from "here to there" but from "there to there."

Using a Field Perspective

We must examine each mission field opportunity from the perspective of the unreached people group still without an evangelical witness. For example, if we are talking about the eleven million unreached Muslims in Bihar State of North India, we must ask ourselves where in India can we recruit missionaries to go to those people?

The first place should be the nearest Christian churches. If we cannot find enough volunteers among the existing churches in Bihar, then we can go next door to West Bengal state and look there. If they are not there, we must go north and south and east and west until we find the nearest church willing to send a missionary team.

Somewhere among India's nearly 100 million believers[5] there are gospel teams who will be able to go among the Bihari Muslims. But is any mission agency from the West actively helping the church in India to mobilize indigenous witness teams to Bihari Muslims? As I write this, there is only one — and their teams have been mobilized at the request of Indian leaders, not by the initiative of the international agency that is helping with support.

The Traditional Answers

Traditional, colonial-era mission agencies offer three solutions to evangelizing unreached people groups such as the Muslims of Bihar. How would each response apply in this situation?

The first response is, *Let's send one of our own from the West.* But this now is impossible, because India will not issue visas to evangelistic missionaries. And the problem is compounded by the fact that Western missionaries are hard to recruit for Muslim work and even harder to support financially.

If that fails, Western missions will next try to *send a missionary social worker, teacher or medical worker to maintain a witness of presence.* India might allow a token teacher or well-digger into Bihar, but no one to witness — and not because the government really needs the outside help. At present there are supposedly 800 to 900 such missionaries in India to reach the whole nation of nearly 940 million souls. Missionary social workers are outnumbered a million to one. No surprise then that their impact on the nation has been minimal to say the least.

Finally, the latest solution being offered is to *send in a foreign tentmaker who will be a part-time witness while holding a secular job.* This has not yet worked in India, since there is little demand for foreign English teachers or outside workers. The government remains opposed to giving work permits to Westerners whom they view as taking jobs away from local citizens.

All three of these solutions attempt to solve the missionary staff problem from a Western perspective and are based on the unspoken assumption that a Western missionary is always the first and best choice. By this kind of thinking, it is considered better to send even a part-time English teacher from the West than to support an Indian citizen who would preach and plant the church working sixteen hours a day for $30 to $45 a month.

To Whom Is the Great Commission Given?

It is critical to understand that Jesus didn't give the Great Commission to a single individual or even to the twelve apostles alone. It was for the whole church as we see in Acts 8:1 and 14. As persecution came, the entire body of believers joined in the evangelization of Judea and Samaria in fulfillment of the Great Commission as recorded in Acts 1:8.

This is an order given to the universal body of Christ as a corporate group. Jesus was telling the *whole* church to take the gospel to the world.

When we see that the call to world evangelism is given to the whole body of Christ, we understand that it is not just something for the affluent churches of the West or even something limited to a class of people called missionaries. We are one unit, and only as we join hands together — black and white, brown and yellow, male and female, Jew and Gentile, clergy and laity — will we be able to accomplish the mission of the church in our generation.

Before we send anyone overseas, we had better get out our maps and see where the nearest local church is. Let's check with the leadership there and see if we can unite our hearts with them to reach their own Judea or Samaria rather than bringing a foreigner in from the outside. There is no biblical reason for us not to fund native missionaries when senders from the indigenous church have used up their resources to support their people going from Jerusalem to Samaria or the uttermost parts. In fact, there are many situations where the local church needs help just to support missionaries to reach millions of local "hidden people" living almost on their doorsteps.

This sending and going relationship is made clear in Romans 10:14-15, where Paul explains that some are called to preach, and others are called to send them. While we send Western missionaries overseas now, most pastors in the West still recognize that we are in the "goer" role at home in our own Jerusalem, Judea or Samaria. But we are at the same time "senders" of other missionaries to the uttermost parts. If we can send white missionaries to them, why can't we send black, brown and yellow missionaries as well?

There is no answer to that question being offered today that is not rooted in racism and sectarianism.

"Anything we think we can do in a foreign country today, the local Christians can do also," said an executive of one mission that sees this need for supporting native missionaries. "And they can do it better at a fraction of the cost."

Notes

[1] Article, "A New Day in Missions," *Christian Mission* (Charlottesville, Va.: Christian Aid, Special Edition, 1987), p. 12.

[2] Unpublished study paper by David B. Barrett, *Global Statistics Summary* (Manila, Philippines: Lausanne II Congress on World Evangelization Statistical Task Force, July 11-20, 1989).

[3] Rudy Barlaan, lecture notes (Dallas, Texas: International Linguistics Center, 1985).

[4] Charles Troutman, *Everything You Want to Know About the Mission Field, But Are Afraid You Won't Learn Until You Get There* (Downers Grove, Ill.: InterVarsity Press, 1977), pp. 72-76.

[5] Although the official government census reflects a figure much smaller than this, a number of key Christian leaders who understand the situation believe the number of Indian believers is actually much greater than reported.

Narcissism
in Missions

Intellectually, sending churches and the Western missions establishment pay lip-service to indigenous missions. For decades now it
has been fashionable to stand on church platforms and say that the
future of the mission enterprise rests on the emerging church, or
emerging missions.

But Western mission publications, posters, bulletin boards and pho-
tography still train the spotlight on the foreign missionary. The emphasis
is all on ourselves. *Our* going. *Our* people overseas. The needs of *our*
missionaries. The stories are always on *our* hardships, risks, health and
welfare. The interest of the Western church is still centered on the lives
and ministries of those it sends or hopes to send — not on those who
must be delivered from the bondage of sin.

How different would our mission program look if we saw the mission
field through the eyes of Jesus? Would we see the pictures of people who
are fabulously rich in comparison to the native missionaries in those
distant lands? Or would we see instead the faces of local citizens who
are suffering and dying to pioneer the gospel in the remote villages,

hospitals, prisons and slums of Asia and Africa?

If we saw missions outreach through His eyes instead of our own, we would see some white faces on our mission maps, but many more faces of brown, black and yellow missionaries.

And we would discover that God already has many harvesters ready and waiting to go into the mission fields. We wouldn't send Americans who can't speak Spanish to Mexico for $50,000 a year while hundreds of Mexican soldiers of the cross don't have the $1,000 a year they need to be effective preachers of the gospel.

How important it is that we view the Great Commission task from a field perspective rather than a sending-church perspective. If we did, the critical need for missionaries overseas would be over in less than a decade.

The Solution to the Personnel Crisis

The entire crisis in missionary staff shortages would be solved almost overnight if we were to assign missionaries from the nearest, existing indigenous missions and local churches.

What would happen if we did this?

First, we would multiply the impact of our funds. In many cases we could deploy thirty to seventy-five native missionaries where we now have only one Western missionary family assigned.

Second, we could start to make a real impact on the twelve thousand unreached people groups — including those in China, India and the Soviet Union.

Third, we could redeploy some Western missionaries to other assignments on the field where their skills and talents are more needed, or to areas where the door is open to foreigners and where they could serve most effectively.

Fourth, we could reassign other Western missionaries to the homeland. Here they could use their overseas experience to become expert advocates of native missionaries and the unreached people groups they have encountered on the foreign fields. One of the biggest needs in the days ahead will be for an army of itinerant missionary leaders to re-educate and interpret what is happening on the field to Western churches, prayer bands and donors.

Fifth, we could also reassign these Western missionaries to expand campus, refugee and other ministries to foreign populations in Western nations. The knowledge of culture, language and people-skills that they have developed on the field could be used to make an even greater impact on foreign visitors and guests in the West.

Sixth, we could save millions of dollars annually in funds and personnel which are now involved in missionary recruiting, administration and fund raising. These funds instead could be sent overseas to support indigenous missionaries and be used to raise up more sponsors for them in the Western churches.

Why Not Include Indigenous Missions?

By now you are probably asking, If native missionaries are so effective, why don't more mission agencies and boards change their policies and start to include them in support programs?

That is perhaps the most puzzling question in mission planning and strategy today — the one every informed Christian leader should be asking at every opportunity.

One interesting leaflet I recently read does such a good job of getting to the real heart of the matter that this book would not be complete without a few paragraphs from it.

"During the decade 1910-1920, many people who had been riding horses began to drive cars. Some became so enthusiastic that they said it was silly to trot along on a horse when you could be riding in a car. Others said the day had come when horses were no longer needed.

"Horse lovers were shocked. What kind of talk was that? Think of all the faithful horses that had carried their masters through heat, cold, rain and snow over the centuries. Are we going to say that their labors were futile?

"Who would dare imply a lack of appreciation for all the horse had done for humanity. It was like throwing out the baby with the bath water. Those who loved traditional things became very critical of the 'new fangled machines' with youthful drivers. They wanted things to stay as they had always been, with horses and carriages.

"Blacksmiths and harness makers were especially hostile. Buggy manufacturers were too, at first, but most soon switched to making car bodies. Slowest of all to change were the military men. At the start of World War I some generals shouted, 'Shut off those infernal machines;

they scare the horses. Wars have always been fought on horseback and they always will be.'

"If all this sounds ridiculous, I wish you could see some of the stacks of letters I have received in the past 20 years. I have been saying that a new era has begun in the history of foreign missions. The only way to do it 100 years ago seemed to be to send representatives of American denominations and mission boards to preach the gospel in foreign countries. But today the situation has entirely changed.

"Now there are hundreds of mission groups in Asia, Africa and Latin America made up of the citizens of those countries. Why try to perpetuate the horse and buggy? A new day is here. I challenge Christians everywhere to stop spending tens of thousands of dollars of God's money unnecessarily to send North Americans overseas. Let's send it instead to some of the excellent indigenous missionary movements that God has raised up among the Christian citizens of Asia, Africa and Latin America."[1]

Change Is Sweeping Missions

It must be said that an increasing number of Western mission agencies are struggling with ways to include native missionaries as equals. However, after generations of discrimination, biased policy rulings and outmoded practices, the changes are coming at a sluggish pace.

It is hard to give up power and prominence when you have held it for decades, as established mission leaders have done. Even when you know your way of life is changing, it is painful to accept it or in some cases even to admit it.

Remember, when the independence and national liberation movements began overseas, almost every foreign mission board had an established policy of racial segregation. Even today many missionary housing policies abroad remain off limits to native Christians.

Until recently few traditional mission agencies were willing to recognize that the post-war years were the dawn of a new age in missions. But, beginning in the mid-1980s, an increasing number of American-based independent foreign missions groups started to support indigenous missions. Many denominations have also experimented on a limited scale with occasional grants to indigenous missions boards and groups, although most funds are still funneled through the traditional channels.

A Time to Share

One would hope that all traditional mission agencies will choose to use their vast resources, networks of contacts and good relations with churches to support indigenous missions. If they would share with needy, native missions, the face of missions would be altered overnight.

Native missions should be viewed as an answer to four centuries of prayer rather than as a competitor for the mission support dollar.

However, despite the signs of increased support for native missions, the overall picture remains grim. For this book, a survey was commissioned to sample 467 leading mission agencies in North America. Of the 44.9 percent that replied, we found that 72, or 34.3 percent, still do not seek to form indigenous mission agencies or societies on the mission field.

Sixty-two percent of those who replied said they supported native workers, but always in the context of an employee relationship or another situation controlled by the foreign mission; 3.5 percent replied with qualified answers.

The reasons given for support or nonsupport reflected the diversity of approaches to the challenge of supporting native workers and the deep suspicions Westerners have when it comes to assisting indigenous missionaries:

About 16.2 percent of the respondents said they consider native missionaries to be part of the indigenous church and therefore do not assist them financially.

About 18.8 percent reported that they support native missionaries only indirectly through block grants to the indigenous church for particular projects or campaigns.

Another 18.3 percent said they support or supplement only native missionary staff members who are salaried employees of the mission.

Approximately 16.6 percent said they would accept nationals as equal members of their mission provided they raised their own support on the field or in another sending country.

A further 8.5 percent said they would support them through sponsorship programs from Western nations.

And 5.5 percent said they considered their relationship with natives a partnership and "shared" with them through supplying free literature or in other unspecified ways.

From the pained replies penciled into the margins of survey forms, it is obvious that supporting native workers is a knotty problem to Western mission leaders. It is one that has not been conclusively decided by any means.

Incidentally, a rather large group of mission executives, 15.8 percent, said the question did not apply to their type of mission work. However, when all is said and done, these surveys show only two conclusive trends.

First, Western missions rarely give funds to native workers; second, when funds are given, it is done with great reluctance and then only for programs or staff controlled by the Western agency.

Traditional mission leaders have most often argued that native missionaries should not be supported by the Western church for six main reasons:

(1) *It would cause Christians in the West to think that their Great Commission obligation is fulfilled by merely sending money overseas.* Thus, it would weaken or even destroy overseas missions because American Christians would lose interest and stop supporting mission work if they were not supporting missionaries from their own denomination or race.

(2) *Supporting native missionaries weakens the indigenous church.* It violates the concept of planting indigenous churches.

(3) *You can't trust them.* Native missionaries are not accountable in the same way traditional missionaries are.

(4) *Native missionaries cannot communicate well* with the sending churches in the West.

(5) *Native missionary leaders will get corrupted by exposure to the affluence and luxury of Western life-styles* when they raise support in the West.

(6) *Native missionaries are not even missionaries* because they often don't cross cultures, and unless you cross cultural lines you are not a true missionary.

Notes
[1] *Those Who Drove Cars Were Against Horses, Right?* (Charlottesville, Va.: Christian Aid Mission, undated).

What Prevents Sharing?

The charges against native missionaries enumerated in the previous chapter are serious indeed. Thus they must be considered carefully. Too much is at risk if funds given for missions are misused — either for traditional mission programs or for native missions. I will first list the charge, then respond to it.

Supporting native missionaries will weaken the overall emphasis on missions in the church because Westerners will stop supporting missions when they are less involved in sending members of their own race and church.

This position has been most effectively argued by Wade Coggins, former general director of EFMA, particularly in a widely quoted and reprinted article from *Evangelical Missions Quarterly* titled "The Risk of Sending Our Dollars Only."

"If our churches give only their money, and not their sons and daughters, our missionary vision will be dead in a generation or less," insists Coggins.[1]

It is true that itinerating missionaries while home on furlough have historically been powerful advocates for overseas missions. However, there is no indication that churches and individuals who have started to sponsor native missionaries have decreased their interest in missions. In fact, just the opposite is true. Believers appear to increase their overall interest in missions after sponsoring natives.

I don't know of any native mission advocates who have ever called for sending dollars only. The need for prayer, communication, information and other kinds of involvement is just as great for indigenous missions as it is for traditional missions.

So, far from spelling the death of missionary vision, a well-run program to support native missionaries will actually increase the awareness and participation of Western Christians in the Great Commission.

To investigate this claim further, we surveyed churches who had taken on native missionary sponsorships through Gospel for Asia. The goal? To see if their overall support for missions had increased or decreased since the decision to support indigenous missions.

The churches were asked to list mission societies they support. The replies showed that most churches involved gave to a wide range of denominational and independent missions. Of the 245 churches that responded, the poll showed 86.9 percent had found their experience supporting native missionaries to be rewarding — and were still supporting native missions.

When asked if the congregation's interest in the Great Commission had increased, decreased or stayed the same, 65 percent said it had increased, 1.3 percent said it had decreased, and 33.6 percent said it had stayed the same.

When asked if their church missions budget had increased, decreased or stayed the same, 65 percent said it had increased, 3.2 percent said it had decreased, and 31 percent said it had stayed the same.

The only conclusion that can be drawn from this survey is that there is no indication whatsoever that supporting native missionaries significantly decreases giving to missions or the interest of the local church in missions. The majority of churches reported both an increase in missions interest and missions giving as a result.

Supporting native missionaries weakens the indigenous church overseas.

The history of this entire argument revolves around the concept of planting indigenous local churches, a theory that had to be introduced about 150 years ago because of the abuses by Western colonial missions who were then dominating the churches they planted.

Western missions created the problem and then came up with an inflexible "solution" that today has become one of the main hindrances to fulfilling the Great Commission.

Although it is not necessarily a biblical concept, the notion of *self-supporting, self-governing* and *self-propagating* churches has been raised by colonial-era Protestant missions to a theological tradition almost as important as the Bible. Therefore, financial aid is rarely if ever given to local indigenous churches or pastors today because it is believed this will spoil the pastors by making them dependent on Western aid.

"What these traditional mission leaders fail to see," says one indigenous mission supporting agency, "is that there is no such thing as a self-supporting mission board or Bible school.

"Hudson Taylor started the China Inland Mission in England, but he also received support from Europe and America. Years later Andrew Gih started the Evangelize China Fellowship in Shanghai; why should he not also receive support from abroad?"

Let's carry this example one step further. Hudson Taylor not only received financial assistance from outside sources, but prayer and moral support as well. His ministry was not weakened by outside support; rather it was *strengthened*. In the same way, the relationships formed through Western support of indigenous missionaries can only serve to bolster and encourage them in the calling God has placed on their lives.

Native missionaries are not accountable to the local church.

In reality, rarely do we find *any* missionaries today being directly accountable to sending churches, whether they are native missionaries or foreign missionaries.

Most missionaries today are primarily accountable to the mission boards and agencies that sponsor them. The majority of native missionaries, like foreign missionaries, also report to formal and informal field councils or eldership boards that hold them accountable for their activities and personal Christian testimonies.

These field-level committees usually report back to mission agencies in the West who in turn report back to the sending churches and donors. This may seem to be a cumbersome process indeed, but it is one that I personally see working effectively on a daily basis.

Therefore, the practical relationship of trust and accountability between the sponsoring group and the missionary actually hinges on *indirect* accountability through committees and boards. It really depends mostly on how much trust the donors have in the home office of the mission agency in the sending country. Few church leaders or mission donors ever travel abroad to inspect the work of the missionary on the field. So they must rely on the network of intermediaries between them and the missionary.

In the homeland or among sending churches, financial accountability is quite easy to establish since most reputable missions offer audited annual reports. Plus many belong to watchdog agencies such as the Evangelical Council for Financial Accountability or the Better Business Bureau or are audited by denominational authorities.

On the mission field, many similar organizations, both formal and informal, are in place and operating. Most mission boards and agencies that adhere to high standards in the United States are working just as hard on the field to ensure accountability from native missionaries. However, accountability standards need to be watched constantly both in the homeland and on the mission field.

Wise donors and sponsoring churches need to exercise vigilance and ask questions, just as they would in any stewardship decision. But there is no reason whatsoever to believe that native missionaries are any less accountable than traditional missionaries.

Can We Trust the Natives?

We entrust native missionaries with only a fraction of the funds we put into the hands of Western missionaries. Yet we are looking for controls and audits we wouldn't dare ask of traditional missionaries.

Meanwhile, there are ample controls, checks and balances on all legitimate native mission work equal or better than what is in place for foreign missionaries.

Sending churches have an obligation and right to be good stewards. They should expect a sound statement of faith, regular reports from the field, including financial reports, and a system of accountability that is consistent with New Testament principles.

This is available if supporting churches and individual donors will establish several policies:

(1) Don't give support directly to missionaries on the field.

(2) Don't start supporting native missionaries on your own, but work with a team of other believers.

(3) Plug into existing mission agencies, especially those who sponsor native missionaries.

(4) Recognize local leadership on the field and never go around them.

(5) Assist existing leaders in extending their vision for their nation rather than funding and financing your own vision.

(6) Examine the fruit of the ministries you support in terms of personal holiness of leaders, souls being saved and new churches being planted.

(7) Minister to native-born citizens of the country you're interested in who are temporarily living in North America, such as students, tourists and businessmen. Get personally involved as a church with immigrants from that mission field who still have relatives back in their homeland.

The Holy Spirit leads us into all truth, and He will guide any sincere individual or church that wants to get involved in assisting native missionaries overseas.

Native missionaries have a difficult time communicating back and reporting on their work to sending churches and donors.

Bonds to the home church and family ties have traditionally been an important part of initial support raising and communication in general. This custom was an important factor in many mainline sending churches and denominations during colonial days. From there it spread to many of the older evangelical churches.

Mission societies that sponsor native missionaries realize they must overcome the lack of expected personal contact and look for new ways to bond sponsors and the missionaries they support. They have discovered it is possible to develop a deep prayer and support relationship between the missionary and his or her senders at home and in the West.

Most of these methods involve strong communications programs. Supporters of native missionaries can receive photographs, testimonies and reports from the field. In addition, mass media tools such as newspapers and videos bring the missionary and the field much closer to sponsors and help make up for the lack of face-to-face visits.

We need not be enslaved to the old methods of mission support raising based on visits from itinerating missionaries. A growing number of native missionary advocates are traveling in North America. These visitors help put the sending churches in closer touch with the field.

Thus, the missions movement is not dependent on visits home from supported missionaries, as cherished as this tradition has become. In fact, mission agencies who want to add native missionary support programs to their ministry can easily do so. It may mean adding different kinds of support-raising programs than have been used in the past, but it can be done.

Western support will corrupt native missionaries by exposing them to the affluence and luxury of Western life-styles.

While it is necessary for a few older native missionary leaders to travel in the West to report on the work and help raise support, I have consistently opposed native missionaries coming to Western nations and itinerating for support. There are two reasons for this.

First, I believe there is a very real danger they will grow too accustomed to Western mores and become less effective when they return to the field. Many native missionaries become filled with pride after visits to the West, and they pick up bad habits that hinder their ministries on the mission field.

Western methods and culture are intoxicating and deceptive to the visitor. Many methods that work well in the West will not transfer into another culture. Many a Western-educated church leader has found rejection and failure when he first returned home and tried to implement the new life-styles and technologies he acquired abroad.

Second, from practical experience, I have found that cross-cultural communication is just as difficult for native missionaries visiting the West as it is for Western missionaries going to Third World nations. Most native missionaries find it difficult to communicate and present their ministries to Western sponsors and congregations. Many go home bitter and confused by the lack of hospitality they experience in Europe and North America. They cannot understand why their ministries and projects are rejected by Western believers. Ironically, most Westerners are not even aware they have offended the visiting native missionary.

So, in this case, the argument against native missionaries working in the West is a valid one. However, in future years it will probably be necessary for more native missionaries to itinerate in the West just as traditional missionaries have. The Western churches need to see the fire and zeal of native leaders firsthand. Also, native missionaries frequently have a message from God for churches in the West.

As this happens, it will be necessary to trust the Holy Spirit to protect and guide these native missionaries just as we have prayed for the protection of traditional missionaries over the years.

Again, the question must be asked: How much of this concern for the native missionary is genuine? It could be that much of the fatherly concern expressed for native missionaries traveling in the United States is really a selfish attempt to protect donor bases. Why isn't this same concern expressed for American missionaries whose salaries are forty to forty-five times higher than native missionaries? Aren't they also exposed to materialism and endangered by the lures and temptations of luxury in the West?

Native missionaries are not really missionaries at all because often they are not cross-cultural; therefore they should not be supported.

Most native missionaries are, in fact, working cross-culturally according to the strict definitions of anthropologists and sociologists. When a Tamil from South India goes to work among Punjabis in North India, it is a completely valid cross-cultural witness (according to the popular concept of cross-cultural evangelism championed as essential by many Western missiologists).

However, there is not a shred of biblical evidence to elevate cross-cultural evangelism to the place it holds today in popular missiology. Certainly, to require that missionaries work cross-culturally is unbiblical and contrary to common sense.

Consider these facts:

• The apostle Paul, a Jew born and raised in a Hellenistic Roman colony, spent his entire missionary career going to other Greco-Roman colonies where he was a natural part of the culture. He spoke the languages and moved freely as a native-born member of both societies.

• From the day of Pentecost, it was foreign visitors to Jerusalem who carried the gospel back to their homes throughout the Roman empire. In reality the gospel spread by immigration and tourism more than intentional cross-cultural witness.

"So what is left?" asks the traditional missionary. "How should the Western church most effectively involve itself in the Great Commission today?"

First, Christians in the West must rediscover the real meaning of the Great Commission. Beginning in our own prayer and devotional lives, we must begin to feel the compassion of the Lord for a lost and dying world. The Great Commission is not something that was given to a tiny group of specially trained and educated envoys. It was given to all Christians — to the whole church. It is something that we are all to be engaged in naturally every day.

Second, involve yourself and your congregation in reaching out to the lost world around you — including foreign students, visitors, refugees and immigrants in your community. Through the aliens in your community who are surrendering their culture to yours, the Lord will open a witness for you to reach out to the globe. And don't forget to witness to your peers and others in your own ethnic community. Establish a balanced witness to your Jerusalem, Judea, Samaria and the uttermost part.

Third, become a sender. Get involved in supporting frontline native missionaries who are working among the unreached people groups. Personally and as a congregation, get involved in sponsoring indigenous missionaries and adopting an unreached people group. Pray for those who can effectively take the gospel to places where you cannot go.

Fourth, go as God calls you. But realize first of all that there is no biblical basis for most of the colonial-style mission activity in operation today.

However, that fact does not preclude you from going overseas for the sake of the gospel. Although colonial-style mission activity often appears spiritually bankrupt, we have many examples of God sending out prophets like Jonah in the Scripture and in history. When God makes such a call on a person's life, it is the obligation of the rest of the body to rally around and send that one into the harvest.

The challenge to the Western church and missions leadership today is to move with the Holy Spirit. We must support the men and women whom the Lord of the harvest is sending into the mission fields of the 1990s and beyond.

Notes

[1]Article by Wade Coggins, "The Risk of Sending Our Dollars Only," *Evangelical Missions Quarterly* (Wheaton, Ill.: Evangelical Missions Information Service Inc., July 1988), pp. 204-206.

Acknowledging the Supernatural

Brother Mathew looked out over the crowd and felt his heart would burst with love for the people before him. It seemed a long time ago when he first encountered these primitive people located in the interior jungles of India's Maharashtra State. Actually it had been only a few years, but the Lord had moved so mightily among them that thousands had turned from animism to serve the living God. Today many of them gathered to hear Mathew share from the Word.

He spoke simply, yet his voice carried the weight of authority. The words were few, but the villagers listened intently as they sat under a makeshift shade-covering of poles and branches.

Suddenly a distant cry was heard. Mathew stopped his preaching and squinted to see a small group of people hurrying toward the meeting place. What was that they were carrying? It looked like a small child. Perhaps he is sick, and they want prayer, thought Mathew.

As the group drew closer, a cry went up: "The child is dead!"

The sobbing parents related the tragedy quickly. The boy had gone to a pond near his home to wash, but slipped and fell in. Four hours went by before anyone noticed he was missing. That's when someone saw his body floating face down in the water.

The stunned parents, who were believers, prayed desperately for their son. But nothing happened. Then they remembered the meetings going on in the nearby village, where Brother Mathew was preaching. "Let us go," the boy's father said simply. "They will pray, and our child will live."

Now the group climbed to the platform where Mathew was standing and placed the lifeless body in his arms. The crowd waited expectantly. "Pastor, pray for the child. The Lord will raise him up."

Mathew looked down at the body he was holding. There was no sign of life. The normally golden brown skin was a pasty yellow; the body was damp and cold.

Brother Mathew called some of the villagers together whom he knew to be strong in their faith. "Come and lay hands on this child, and we will pray."

As they gathered around the still body, Mathew prayed, "Lord! In this situation, let the faith of these people be established by Your miracle. Let Your name be glorified."

Minutes went by as the group prayed for life to return to the little child. Then Mathew felt something, a slight stirring. Could it be? He dared not open his eyes as the group continued to pray. But the movement was unmistakable. He looked down as the boy in his arms started to cry!

"Glory to God!" shouted Mathew. "The child is alive!" The crowd erupted with joy, and the parents were reunited with their son.

The rest of the day became a spontaneous praise service to the living God. Those simple villagers had seen a mighty act of God performed before their very eyes. This miracle was related again and again in that area, and wherever it was shared people believed and turned from their idol worship and pagan ways.

Why the Silence?

This incident is only one of thousands that are occurring on the mission field daily. In these countries, whenever the gospel of the kingdom is preached along with signs and wonders, people are repenting of their sins and turning to Christ. Is there a secret to these success stories? Simply this: Mathew and the thousands like him are following the example of Jesus and His believers in the New Testament.

Jesus' ministry was characterized by the miraculous. Matthew 9:35 says, "And Jesus went about all the cities and villages, teaching in their synagogues, and preaching the gospel of the kingdom, and healing every sickness and every disease among the people." Wherever Jesus went He healed the sick and cast out demons.

When Jesus commissioned His disciples to go and preach in Matthew 10:8, He told them to "heal the sick, cleanse the lepers, raise the dead, cast out devils: freely ye have received, freely give." These signs were evidence of the gospel of the kingdom.

All five renderings of the Great Commission in the New Testament make a clear reference to the promised divine authority and supernatural power that will accompany the preaching of the gospel. In fact, the Lord Jesus specifically forbade His disciples to undertake the Great Commission until they had received the promised power from the Holy Spirit. With it came the authority to proclaim the gospel with compelling conviction as first demonstrated at Pentecost.

After Jesus ascended to heaven and His followers received the promised Holy Spirit, they went everywhere preaching the kingdom of God, casting out demons and healing the sick in His name. The book of Acts continues the exciting story of how the Great Commission was carried out in the first century.

Yet when these same wondrous endorsements of gospel preaching occur on the mission field *today*, a strange silence descends over Western mission gatherings.

Dan Whitby of Bible Translations on Tape asserts that most Western missionaries are actually afraid to acknowledge them publicly. When they come home on furlough, they often are careful not to discuss or report the miracles that are regularly occurring on the mission field.

In the article "Discovering the Living God," he writes, "It is a shame that so many missionaries feel stifled and unable to share the wonders they see the living God performing overseas. In most mission publications and at conferences, there is a studied effort to downplay the supernatural.

"Why is this? Many missionaries fear their reports won't be believed or even that prayer and financial support will be lost if they share miracle stories. Many fear they will become labeled as fanatics.

"What specifically am I talking about? Actually, nothing more extraordinary than the supernatural events that were a normal part of the New Testament. God's people through the ages have routinely seen miracles, healing, casting out of demons, resurrections, dreams and visions. Angelic visitations and supernatural supply are commonplace in Scripture.

"You see, God is doing mighty things around the world today. As His people invade enemy territory, simple believers often see answers to prayer as in the Gospels and Acts. The living God is supporting His servants as they establish the kingdom of God in the hearts of lost millions.

"But the philosophies of scientific rationalism have captured the hearts and minds of Western societies. Like a cancer, this unbelief has even spread into the churches of North America."[1]

Yet the promise of power and authority and the enabling of the Holy Spirit are mentioned in nearly every rendering of the Great Commission. Jesus promised that His missionaries would have such a supernatural endorsement on their ministry.

Why Are We Afraid to Admit Our Need of His Power?

Could it be that most Western missionaries, educated into unbelief and powerlessness, are afraid to acknowledge miracles because it reveals their own spiritual weaknesses?

Is the sin of spiritual pride keeping some of God's choice servants defeated and impoverished in their spiritual warfare?

Why would anyone not want the miracle power that Jesus promised to missionary witnesses? Without it, how else could one ever come against the spiritual forces that hold the harvest fields in bondage? How else does one handle spiritual ignorance and fear built up over centuries? And how would one handle the inevitable encounters with demons?

Missions is not applied anthropology, comparative religion and sociology. It is storming the gates of hell. It is a power confrontation — hand-to-hand combat with Satan and his demons.

Consider, for example, this true account of a missionary experience in Sri Lanka. How else could it have been faced unless the Lord Himself intervened along New Testament lines?

This situation occurred in the life of a native missionary. He is now a church-planting evangelist supported by Gospel for Asia.

Before turning his life over to the Lord Jesus, Harath Bandula was a prominent member of a prosperous Buddhist business family. He, along with twelve other members of his immediate family, operated several successful firms based in the village of Teldeniya near Kandy. But their wealth provoked envy and jealousy from others in the community.

In 1974 spiteful neighbors and distant relatives hired a local "Kattadiya" witch doctor to cast a spell over the family. As a result two members of the family were plagued with visits from strange, evil powers. In order to free themselves from the black magic, the family retained their own Kattadiya medium. Like millions of other Sri Lankans do daily, they consulted astrologers to help search for a charm that would successfully break the curse.

But their efforts to fight witchcraft with witchcraft failed. After spending the family savings on the most famous astrologers and sorcerers in the nation, they were told that nothing could be done. In fact, a leading astrologer predicted that the strange series of misfortunes would eventually take the lives of all twelve family members!

Signs of demonic activity in the family homestead became more frequent. Their once comfortable and peaceful life-style turned into a nightmare. Strange sounds and voices could be heard when no one was present. Unidentifiable and vaporous figures would appear walking in the house and garden.

It was like a scene from a horror movie. Everybody's worst nightmares seemed to be coming true, and townfolk began to believe that their house was haunted.

Physical objects moved. Glass and pottery shattered. The garden would be littered immediately after being swept clean. Money disappeared from inside locked boxes. Family members were living on the verge of hysteria and madness.

Then the demonic attacks became violent and threatening. The demons would possess various members of the family in turn, causing them to attempt suicide. Terrible faces and forms would appear in windows and throughout the house — spirit manifestations with unkempt hair, bared teeth and tongues dripping blood.

Another sympathetic Kattadiya made an attempt to "cut" the knot of the curse, and his wife immediately died. Disillusioned, and overcome by the evil powers he could no longer manipulate, he gave up witchcraft. Now the family was left completely on its own to fight the spiritual attacks in any way it could.

They pilgrimaged to nearby temples, appealing to Buddha. But it was to no avail. They wrote for advice to a leading astrological newspaper and received a confirmation that the spell was irrevocable. The newspaper's advice column said the omens and signs were very negative. The entire family was "doomed for destruction" on July 10, the medium asserted.

God Answers a Plea for Deliverance

Finally, the eldest son determined to offer his body to a benevolent spirit for possession, hoping that the malevolent forces would flee. This plan failed as well. Then he remembered a correspondence course he had taken from a Bible school in the capital. In desperation he wrote and asked for help from the Christian God since everything else had failed.

Touched by the plea, a student from the Bible school and a local pastor came to visit the family on July 7, three days before the deadline predicted by the fortune-tellers. No sooner had they knocked on the door than a demon in one of the women of the family screamed out in recognition and horror at the presence of Jesus in the missionaries.

The woman fled to a nearby cemetery where she was found later, hiding among the tombs like the Gadarene demoniac in Luke 8:26-39. She was so violent it took several men to restrain her and bring her back to the house.

But the native missionaries prayed and took the authority that was theirs in Jesus Christ. The powers of darkness were overcome by a power greater then they and were cast out in the name of Jesus Christ. The grip of fear and death over the family was broken through the prayers of two of God's faithful servants. Not only was the woman delivered from the demons, but the rest of the clan members were set free as well.

Eventually every member of the family became a born-again Christian, and many in that area have come to believe in Christ. There have been no more demonic manifestations in the house. When the haunting began, there were no Christians in the village. Today there are forty Buddhist converts in Teldeniya. Weekly worship services are now held in what was once a haunted house, and the Christian witness as a result of this deliverance is known for miles around.

Young Harath was converted and answered the call for full-time

Christian service. He went on to Bible school and is now a powerful preacher and witness throughout the large Buddhist community in Sri Lanka.

Warfare in the Heavenlies

No veteran missionary would be surprised to hear this kind of report. Yet Ken Baker, an SIM International missionary to Africa, explains what it is like to serve on the mission field armed only with a rational, Western education:

"One time in Monrovia, Liberia, a young fellow in my discipleship group came to see me. He wanted to return to his village to see his mother, but he had learned that his uncle had placed a curse on him because he had become a Christian and would no longer participate in the bush (Poro) society. In view of his fear and nervousness, we prayed briefly, and I told him that he did not need to worry about the curse because he was a believer in Jesus. (My response still haunts me.) However, my answer did not satisfy him.

"I did not see him again for more than three months. When he came back, he told me that he had become extremely ill and almost died. All along, he had feared that he would never leave the village alive. Well, I thought, he must have drunk some contaminated water or something. With my Western scientific worldview, I interpreted the events the only way I knew how, by rational deduction. But this incident, and many others like it, forced me to conclude that my teaching and counseling were totally inadequate.

"My experiences in West Africa forced me out of my naivete, because I had to reckon with the obvious presence of demonic power and the fear it generated....I came to realize how much Western rationalism had clouded my understanding of the spirit world."[2]

Encounters with supernatural powers of evil are routine on the mission fields of the Third World. The Gospel for Asia offices receive reports nearly every day that sound exactly like pages from the book of Acts. And these are not emotional experiences whipped up in the frenzy of a mass meeting. Such miracles are performed by the Lord quietly through native missionaries who know how to exercise their God-given authority over the powers of Satan as explained throughout the Gospels and the New Testament.

When Christ commissioned the seventy disciples, He told them, "Heal the sick that are therein, and say unto them, The kingdom of God is come nigh unto you" (Luke 10:9). When a healing took place, it was visible evidence of the kingdom of God entering into that village. Today, in the remote, unreached corners of the world, when a miracle is performed, it is still a dramatic testimony to the power of God conquering the forces of darkness.

Over the years, respected native missionary leaders have witnessed many such supernatural victories by the forces of light over darkness. We have found that such miraculous manifestations of the Holy Spirit almost always occur in conjunction with large movements of whole families and villages toward salvation in Christ.

Jesus told His disciples that the only way to capture enemy territory for the kingdom of God is to bind the strongman (Luke 11:20-22). The only way to gain victory over the powers of darkness — and thus fulfill the Great Commission — is to conquer each stronghold through the demonstration of the power of God.

This kind of authoritative witness is essential on most mission fields, lands where evil manifestations of demon power are routine. Billions of people are still held captive to idol and spirit worship, beginning and ending their days with ritual offerings. They burn incense and sacrifice the living to satiate the horrible spirits that animate their idols.

Even the most benevolent of demon spirits require ceremonial worship and offerings on a regular basis. So it should not surprise us to discover that Satan will not loosen his grip of terror unless the gospel is preached powerfully in word and deed. For millions of people enslaved in spiritual darkness, they must see evidence of something better and stronger than their idol gods and shrines. Only this will give them courage to cast off their chains of bondage to folk religion.

Western Missions' Response to the Supernatural

One of the saddest legacies of Western-style colonialism on the mission field today is rationalism and unbelief in the power of the supernatural. As a result most traditional missionaries and their converts are powerless to deal with common demonic attacks.

Colonial missionaries, whether sent by liberal denominations or evangelical faith missions, were deeply affected by nineteenth- and twentieth-century worship of science and technology. Humanistic beliefs in the ultimate goodness and supremacy of man left the church and missions with a bankrupt theology.

This philosophy left no theological foundation for the living God of the Bible, who is an active partner in the enterprise of outreach and Christian witness.

It is no surprise, then, to find that modern missions seek to duplicate the healing miracles of Jesus and the apostles by opening hospitals. This attempt to imitate the liberating light of the gospel by starting schools and hospitals can bring only limited benefits. Because this gospel is not the true good news of Jesus Christ, it lacks power to change people and societies.

Neither is it any surprise that often evangelical missionaries rule out the possibility of divine intervention in the everyday challenges of the mission field. Such missionaries are going out to proclaim salvation. But if they do not demonstrate their message of hope when they face the inevitable victims of demon possession and illness that characterize heathen lands, their message is weak and often futile. By their teaching, the living God became inactive in human affairs following the last chapter of Acts.

Brad Hill, an Evangelical Covenant missionary to Zaire, shares his experience of this truth:

"Something else I learned from the African people is the reality of the spirit world. There *is* a whole demonic spirit world that I didn't learn about at seminary....I didn't learn about exorcisms and healing and casting out demons. I haven't learned a lot of that yet, but I am very aware of the whole different realm of life. I want to talk to my students about the authorship of Hebrews, but my students want to know how Paul cast out demons. These people are teaching me what the Scripture means when it says that 'the Kingdom of God is upon you.' It certainly refers to more than I have experienced. These people know something about the battle between the kingdom of darkness and the kingdom of light. They know what it is like to have Christ present and to see people healed and demons cast out."[3]

With the exception of a handful of missionaries who first appeared in the 1920s, few colonial-era missionaries expected to preach a gospel that would be backed up by the Holy Spirit with the signs and wonders referred to in Acts 5:12. For the most part they succeeded in branding the few Pentecostals who appeared as "divisive" and "fanatical" — thus avoiding a painful confrontation with the fact that their own ministries were powerless and ineffective.

Notes

[1]Article by Dan Whitby, "Discovering the Living God," *The Vision* (Cedar Hill, Tex.: Bible Translations on Tape, Vol. I, No. 2, Fall 1989), p. 7.

[2]Article by Ken Baker, "Power Encounter and Church Planting," *Evangelical Missions Quarterly* (Wheaton, Ill.: Evangelical Missions Information Service, July 1990), pp. 308-311.

[3]Article, "Door Interview: Brad Hill," *The Wittenburg Door* (Yreka, Calif.: Youth Specialties, February-March 1987), pp. 22-27.

When God Performs
Miracles, People Believe

How unlike the God of the Bible is the Jesus preached and worshipped by many Western missionaries on the field today. Instead of a living God who invades the present and demonstrates Himself through His servants, they too often present the world with a God more like a neatly sealed-up package.

This is the god of the modern, Western church. He is functional, easy to understand and nonobtrusive. He is always there when you feel like using him for a little comfort, but otherwise he stays politely out of the way. Once, long ago, in the days of the prophets or during apostolic times, this god was alive and active in the affairs of men. But now he has retired and left the church without his ongoing presence and power.

This inadequate concept presents us with a false image of God. He saves souls from hell but then leaves us to our own wits and skills to live the Christian life on this earth. This god is in reality a man-made idol. Such an inept concept of God is found nowhere in Scripture. And certainly such a powerless God is not the God of kingdom authority who promised us we would receive *power from the Holy Spirit to fulfill the*

Great Commission.

Why is it so important for Western seminary professors, theologians and churchmen to fight the miraculous? Instead of denying the supernatural or substituting Western technology, theology and doctrines, the Western church must submit to the power of the living God.

The mission world today is bulging with statistics of all kinds. One can pick and choose mission and church-planting theories like the varieties of soda pop in a vending machine. There are enough available courses and seminars on "Reaching the Unreached" to make your head swim.

The mind-set of Western society today, and even the main trend in the majority of our Western churches, is measurement of individuals, events and even spiritual matters by scientific rationalism. Education, logic and mental ability have become interwoven with everything we are and everything we do. We encourage prospective missionaries to educate themselves as fully as possible, assuring them that then they will be fully equipped.

We can study maps, expound theories and juggle statistics all we want — but *until we experience the power of God in our ministries, there is little chance for eternal fruit.*

A.W. Tozer, in his classic book *Paths to Power*, puts an accusing finger on one of the most vexing problems in the world of missions today.

"No one with a knowledge of the facts can deny the need for supernatural aid in the work of world evangelization. We are so hopelessly outclassed by the world's superior strength that for us it means either God's help or sure defeat. The Christian who goes out without faith in 'wonders' will return without fruit. No one dare be so rash as to seek to do impossible things unless he has first been empowered by the God of the impossible. 'The power of the Lord was there' is our guarantee of victory."[1]

Encounters With Evil Forces

Effective missionary work occurs when we renounce our own wisdom and methodology and go out to witness for Jesus with the anointing and power of the Holy Spirit. When this is done, we find ourselves like Elijah confronting the prophets of Baal on Mount Carmel. God comes down to earth and vindicates His true servants — sending consuming fire onto the altar.

Brother Mathew shares one of the many "Mount Carmel experiences" he has confronted:

"When I went to one village for the first time, preaching that Jesus Christ is the one true God, a group of men came up to me, followed by a bullock cart. A man was lying in the cart, and I could see that he was very ill, perhaps on the point of death. His friends had heard of my preaching, and they thought I was bringing another god to be added to the ones they already had in their tribal villages.

"They told me, 'This man has been bedridden for three weeks, and he is dying. We have brought him ten miles on this bullock cart. If your God is the true God, then this man should be healed. You stop your preaching and you pray to this new God for our friend.'

"Then the ultimatum came: 'Either he will stand up, completely well, right now — and we will take you to our village and hear about this God — or, if he dies tonight, we will drive you out. You cannot escape from our hands.'

"Quickly I prayed: 'Lord, You are the living God. Let Your power be displayed so that these people may believe.'

"Before I could even open my eyes, this man threw the blanket that had been covering him out of the cart. He asked for his walking stick and began to stand up shakily. The Lord gave me great boldness, and I shouted, 'Throw away your stick and jump from the cart!' He tossed his cane away, jumped out of the cart and walked to the platform where I was standing.

"The next morning our team was taken to his village and received like kings! The people believed the Word of God, and a great number were saved. This is how a large chain of churches was started in that area — through the healing of this one man."

In the interior villages of North India, in the jungles of Africa, in the tribal areas of Indonesia — people are not going to be won to Christ through ideological, philosophical arguments. The kingdom of darkness is ruling the lives of millions of people today who live in places like these. All of our abilities, arguments and theories will never set these people free. There has to be a demonstration of the power of God — a direct confrontation with the forces of darkness.

The people who live in our generation are just like those who lived in Jesus' day. If those people were given signs, wonders and miracles by the Lord Jesus Christ as proof of His deity, I believe that those lost and dying millions who live with unbelief in our generation *also* need to see and experience the power of God in their own lives. Only in this way will they be drawn to Jesus and have eternal life.

A well-known evangelist and missionary has said, "I am fully convinced that on the mission field today, one mighty miracle in the name of the Lord Jesus Christ among Hindus, Muslims, Buddhists or animists is worth more than a lifetime of preaching theory and philosophy."

I have experienced this principle in my own life, I've seen it applied in Brother Mathew's ministry, and I've seen it repeated time and time again in thousands of brothers we serve on the mission fields of Asia.

Throwing ourselves upon God and believing in Him to endorse our witness in this manner has a powerful effect on lost souls. It often opens doors long closed to the gospel and is the first step in winning families, tribes and even whole villages to Christ.

Daughter's Healing Opens Closed Village

The power of God often breaks open villages that have been closed to any kind of Christian witness for centuries.

Hari Vithal Shinde was born and raised in a small Hindu village in Maharashtra, India. Until he attended a gospel meeting in a nearby village, he sacrificed to spirits and worshipped the village idols just as his family and friends did, and as their ancestors had for countless generations.

But after hearing the plan of salvation, Hari turned from his life of rebellion and followed Christ. The decision terrified his family, who begged him to keep his new faith a secret. However, he kept on witnessing and threw all the family idols out of the house in a dramatic demonstration of his faith.

This act enraged the villagers, and Hari was driven out of town by the angry elders. For over a year he was not allowed to come back. During that time he went from village to village throughout the surrounding district sharing the good news of salvation with anyone who would listen. His life of holiness and sacrifice became well-known in the meantime — even to those in his home village who had forced him to wander homeless for Jesus.

But then the daughter of the village leader became deathly ill. The doctors gave up all hope, and the same elder who had cursed Hari now sent a messenger asking him to come back and pray for the girl.

"When I prayed," recalls Hari, "God healed that little girl completely, and this opened the way for me to come back to my village. The leader told me I could preach my Jesus, and eleven people came to the Lord."

Since then many others in the village and surrounding areas have shown interest in Jesus. Hari has dedicated the rest of his life to establishing local churches throughout that part of India.

Five Hundred Come to Jesus in Bangladesh Village

James Sangma, a native missionary in Bangladesh, grew up in a Hindu village of that predominantly Muslim nation. He tells the remarkable story of a healing miracle in his home village that resulted in the conversion and public baptism of more than five hundred people!

His family and village worshipped a terrifying Hindu god which they carved from bamboo.

One day an itinerant evangelist came to a village where Sangma was working. "As the evangelist was preaching," he recalls, "I realized that this was the most wonderful message I had ever heard in my life. The love of Jesus touched me deeply, and that night I gave up all my idols and accepted Jesus as the true God and my Savior. My life was completely changed. I was publicly baptized, and I worshipped the Lord along with other believers. I found the peace and joy I had longed for over many years."

But Sangma feared to return to his home village, knowing that his new faith in Jesus would make him the object of hatred and scorn.

Finally, however, he made a trip home. There he announced to parents, relatives and friends his decision to follow Christ. An angry mob formed and tried to force him to worship the village god at a sacred tree in the center of the village. But Sangma refused and was finally forced to leave the village and seek work elsewhere.

During this period he began to feel the call of God on his life and a burden to go back to his own people to establish a church. After attending Bible school for two years, he returned home, but again the village shunned him. He became an outcast, and even his own family refused to accept him back.

Then a young boy in the village became seriously ill. The family of the boy hired Hindu priests to pray and call publicly upon the idol to save their son. Each day the boy grew worse as the family begged and pleaded for healing at the sacred tree. But the idol was deaf to the sacrifices and cries of the family.

One day, as they entreated favor from their demon god, Sangma asked the grieving family to give him a chance to pray to the living God. "I prayed over the boy," says Sangma, "and commanded him in the name of Jesus to get up."

The boy stood up, started talking and asked for something to eat. He was completely well. "The people standing around immediately believed on Jesus Christ, having just seen His wonderful love and power," says Sangma.

Today a strong church exists in that village, and Sangma has gone on to witness and establish more churches in the tribal areas of India's Assam State.

Rain Showers and Deliverance Start Thai Churches

Lun Poobuanak, a hard-working native missionary working with Buddhists and animists in Kalasin Province, Thailand, saw an entire village of 134 families turn to Christ after God answered his prayers for rain.

The confrontation came one Sunday morning while he was holding services for a tiny group of Christians in one village. Although it was rainy season, the monsoon had not yet come, and the crops were only days away from ruin. The village was in despair, and during the service village leaders came in and interrupted the prayers with a strange offer.

"If you ask your God to give us rain this month, all 134 households in our clan will worship your God and become Christians," said the *mooban*, or head man.

"At first," says Lun, "I rebuked them for trying to play games with the living God, but they insisted that they were serious."

"We vow to become Christians," said the mooban. "If we do not, your God can send judgment on us."

So Lun and the Christians gathered together for three days of prayer and fasting, asking God to send rain. On the fourth day a cloudburst came that flooded all the klongs (canals) and rice fields. "The rain was so intense," says Lun, "that the villagers humbly admitted that Jesus is the only true and living God in the universe."

Word of the miracle storm spread to many surrounding districts, and all 134 households converted to Christ as well as others. "This is a living testimony that still helps us to win souls easily in this area," says Lun.

In another incident related by native missionary Soontawn Rawang in Buriram Province near the Khmer border of Thailand, a demon-possessed girl pointed her village toward salvation. In this region the people were pure spirit worshippers, believing that both good and evil demons possessed certain trees, rocks, mountains, rivers and even people.

In one area an evil spirit was very strong and much-respected by the villagers. It was so feared that everyone believed those who refused to sacrifice to it would get sick and die. There were many stories of local people who became ill after mocking or joking about this particular spirit.

The native missionaries prayed and fasted before going to the village for an evangelistic crusade because they knew the grip this demon had on the hearts of the local people. What they didn't realize was that the landlord and his daughter who rented them their meeting hall were mediums for the spirit.

During the meeting the demon spoke out through the landlord's daughter, saying that he didn't like the Christians visiting the area. The demon went on to insist that the Christians be forbidden to preach Jesus in the village.

Before the crowd could act against the missionaries, however, Soontawn and the gospel team rebuked the demon using Mark 16:17-20 as their authority. They cast the demon out of the girl as the awestruck villagers watched in fear and trembling. In the following days the missionaries went from house to house without harm in the area. Soon many others in the village came forward asking that demons be cast out.

Within a month there were nine separate church groups formed in the district, all as a result of deliverance from demon spirits in the area.

Livestock Healed in India

In Maharashtra, India, two different native missionaries write telling how miracle healings of livestock have turned families and villages to faith in Christ.

Dhyanoba Pandurang Kotambe and his wife were devout Hindus when they heard the gospel and decided as a couple to forsake the gods of their village and follow Christ. Immediately there was agitation to excommunicate them from the village, although the threats were not carried out.

One day soon after, Dhyanoba was asked by his Hindu neighbor to say a prayer for a sick buffalo. To his complete surprise God miraculously healed the animal, and news of the incident spread quickly throughout the village.

"This incident brought a great change in our society," writes Dhyanoba, "and many people became interested in knowing more about Jesus as a result."

At the time this testimony was recorded there were fifteen converts in the village, and a small congregation had been formed.

In a similar incident related by native missionary Ranba Sambaji Gaikwad, a Hindu man dared him to pray for a sick bull.

"If your God heals this bull, I will worship Him," he challenged.

"I prayed a simple prayer," recounts Ranba, "and the bull was completely healed. That man was astonished. He stopped worshipping all other gods and started coming to the Christian worship services."

The Heart of True Missionary Work

Whole volumes could be filled with stories from our files of how individuals, families and entire villages have been converted as a result of one healing or miraculous answer to prayer. Often such inexplicable signs and wonders are the spark that sets off a whole chain of conversions.

The witness of simple believers relying on the power of God is at the heart of all successful missionary work. As you witness these miracles and hear stories from native missionaries around the world, you cannot help but be struck at how similar their accounts are to the stories in the Gospels and the book of Acts. This is probably because new expectations and faith levels are actually being created by reading the Word of God.

"Faith cometh by hearing," says Paul, "and hearing by the word of God" (Rom. 10:17).

The exploding church and mission movements of Africa, Asia and Latin America are discovering the Bible and taking it at face value. Jesus exercised authority over devils, and so are they. Nobody has told them anything different — or yet explained these miracles away — and so thousands of simple native missionaries are moving across the map with apostolic power.

Native missionaries often come from cultures where territorial spirits, powers and demon authorities are taken for granted. While Western theologians write books and articles against the idea that there are spiritual powers that need to be bound, simple-minded Asian missionaries are claiming territory for God and planting churches deeper and deeper in enemy territory.

When will we learn this lesson? Why is the power of God still a taboo subject in so many of our modern missions programs?

Could it be that we've allowed our fear of extremism, emotionalism and abuse of these gifts to prevent us from exercising one of our most powerful tools in evangelism?

We need to stop over-analyzing these so-called power gifts when we see them practiced on the mission field. Most of all we need to stop slapping labels on native missionaries when we find them demonstrating such supernatural powers in their evangelistic outreach.

If we are going to see the Great Commission fulfilled in our generation, we must rediscover the simple fact that signs and wonders followed the New Testament disciples and were part and parcel of their everyday witness for Christ. Hebrews 13:8 says, "Jesus Christ [is] the same yesterday, and today, and for ever." All that Jesus ever was, He still is now. He still lives, and He is calling people to Himself, proving who He is through miracles just as He did in the New Testament. Until we realize how sidetracked much of the missions world has become in this area of thinking and return to the original pattern Jesus set for us, we will never get the job done.

Let us repent of our unbelief and allow the Holy Spirit to move in our ministries just as He is doing in so many thousands of native missionaries in the Third World.

We should remind ourselves of what happened when Uzzah reached out to steady the ark. It can be fatal to substitute our wisdom and planning for obedience to the simple plans and power of God.

———————————

Notes

[1]A.W. Tozer, *Paths to Power* (Camp Hill, Penn.: Christian Publications, undated), pp. 12-13.

Discovering
the Right Priorities

Why do we so often come up with the wrong answers to the most critical questions in missions strategy today? The reason is simple. When you begin by asking the wrong question, you almost always get the wrong answer.

Nowhere in the Christian world is this more true than in the matter of funding missionary causes. Correctly financing the Great Commission should not be nearly the problem it has become. Once a pastor, a missions committee or even a prayerful individual begins asking the correct questions, correct solutions follow rapidly.

Christians have the common sense to make these right decisions about mission priorities provided they are given the truth about current conditions on the mission field.

"For years I knew there was something fundamentally wrong with our approach to missions," confessed a leading pastor in one evangelical denomination, "but I just couldn't put my finger on it."

His church is nationally known. It has been giving generously to traditional mission programs for decades. In his heart, however, the pastor knew the task of world evangelism simply wasn't getting done. In fact, after a lifetime of faithfully supporting traditional missions, all he could see was that his denomination's missionaries were falling steadily behind in reaching the world.

One Pastor's Discovery

Although most denominational boards and mission agencies are faced privately with mounting evidence of the ineffectiveness of their cross-cultural missions, few local pastors have any way of knowing the true extent of this ongoing disaster in world evangelism.

But this pastor is one of the privileged few who has traveled to a number of mission fields, so he was aware of the eroding respect Western missionaries have overseas. He stayed as a guest in a number of missionary homes and saw the radical gap in life-style between the local population and his missionaries. He realized that if he lived a similar extravagant life-style back home — one that separated him so far from his congregation — he would soon be without a pulpit.

He found that host governments, even those generally friendly to the West, continue to keep their doors closed to missionaries. They were unwanted despite the free social services they often provided.

Meanwhile, soaring populations grow faster. In terms of percentage, foreign missionaries are playing a smaller and smaller role in the overall effort.

Moreover, the strength of traditional, pagan religions seems unaffected by the presence of Western missionaries. Many grow stronger in reaction to the foreign presence of white missionaries. Saddest of all, the number of unreached people groups being touched by Western missionaries has remained almost unchanged for years.

Pastor Hoskins (not his real name) saw all this, so he began to look at the missionary personnel problem from other angles. Finally, after one particularly discouraging trip to the mission field, he approached his missions committee and posed a radically different question.

Seek a Field Solution First

Instead of asking the classical question, "How are *we* going to evangelize the world?" he began to ask, "How are *they* going to hear the gospel?"

What a change in perspective that makes! It frees up mission sponsors to get behind the strategies, people and programs that are actually working.

Instead of centering his missions outreach on how the church could continue sending more people from here to there, Pastor Hoskins was able to start looking at the challenge of world evangelism from the mission field perspective.

Since the church already exists in some form in almost every country, the challenge facing the Western church is a simple one. The sending church needs only to identify who is best reaching out to pioneer areas with the resources they already have.

Once this is done, the church needs to come alongside that board or mission and give them the help for which they ask.

The questions that need to be asked should sound like these: *Who is winning souls on such and such a mission field right now — and what do they say we can do to help them?* Phrased another way, we should ask, *Who is successfully planting churches, and what do they say they need in order to finish the task?*

Some Surprise Answers

The answers to these questions were real shockers to Pastor Hoskins and his board. They were devout Christian leaders who had grown up in a typical evangelical church, and the colonial-style missions mind-set was the only one they'd known.

They loved their missionaries and the comfortable routine of missions conferences and furlough visits from old friends. However, after studying the reality of the field, they discovered they had to rethink their whole missionary support policy.

First, Pastor Hoskins found that *on most mission fields today the only missionaries who are still winning souls and planting churches are native missionaries.* In nations where there are great revivals and people movements, the leaders are inevitably men of the soil who are born and raised among the people they serve.

In fact, he couldn't find one field where a Western missionary was leading a major people movement or planting multiple congregations. As a pastor, it seemed to him that that should be a missionary's first order of business. But Western missionaries he talked to usually admitted they were unsuitable for this primary task and left it to the national church.

Second, he found that *the tools which indigenous missionaries really need and want are usually not even on the list of the average Western missionary.* They desperately need bicycles rather than Land Rovers; cassette tapes rather than floppy disks; rice for their children rather than private English schools.

The technologies still most requested are not medicine, rural development or computer services. These systems are being imposed on the Third World without any help from the Western church. More needed are old-fashioned slide and film projectors, generators, flannelgraph lessons, World War II-era bullhorns, flip-chart teaching posters and basic Christian literature of all kinds.

These simple, inexpensive tools are what indigenous missionaries can use immediately with little or no training. What's more, they create no cultural shock waves when they are used by native missionaries in the homes and rural villages of the Third World.

A Tragic Error

By chaining missions programs to the presence of Western personnel, Pastor Hoskins discovered his church had actually blocked these needed resources from reaching frontline native missionaries.

One of the tragedies of the current situation is that some of the biggest obstacles to completing the Great Commission are the people who should be helping the most. Too often they invest resources in personal comfort and pet programs rather than share with native leaders.

Again and again, thoughtful pastors and lay leaders like Pastor Hoskins are finding that their biggest challenge is discovering ways to get around the old mission bureaucracies! They want to transfer their aid to effective native leaders, but it is painful to confront old classmates and friends with the facts they have learned.

As one of the leaders of his denomination, Pastor Hoskins also feels an obligation to support his foreign mission board and the independent missions that have cultivated support from his church. Several of the members on his missions committee are former missionaries themselves who are deeply committed to continue support to their colleagues in traditional missions.

So today his church is operating a dual program. They are supporting a large number of effective indigenous missionaries, as well as the usual traditional missionaries.

Finding the Cutting Edge

However, it is the native missionaries, says Pastor Hoskins, who are leading the way to unreached people groups, winning souls and planting pioneer churches.

Pastor Hoskins and his missions committee have found that traditional mission structures are holding the real work of the Great Commission captive in two principal ways:

They tend to block funding of critical needs on the field. Western mission structures often siphon off much-needed funds and channel them into personal support or secondary programs that at best have only an indirect effect on world evangelism.

The sad truth is that many of these Western mission programs are no longer having even an indirect impact on fulfilling the Great Commission. Yet these programs absorb the funds sent abroad by most churches and mission societies in the West.

Many of these programs, based on Western institutions, are focused on maintaining the established church structure rather than outreach evangelism. Others focus on economic development, medicine, social services and welfare.

Even more sad is the fact that few Western mission societies have fostered and trained indigenous Christians to take their places. Because they did not treat the nationals as their equals — educated, able and gifted though they were — there are no godly, capable brothers on the field to carry on the work. On scores of fields where translation and tribal evangelism are of paramount importance, missions like these have failed to replicate themselves.

In India, Myanmar, Nepal and Tibet, for example — where translation work and tribal outreach are vitally needed — these missions have failed to develop indigenous agencies to carry on their stated purpose. And what about China and Soviet Asia?

They have created an almost total monopoly on providing news and information in the Western church. The story of native missions is not being told effectively in the Western church press. The resulting picture is a highly distorted one. Native missionaries are often presented as inferior or nonexistent, and the mission field itself is presented through a propaganda screen designed primarily to assist in the fund-raising programs of mission agencies.

Thus you have situations in which unreached people groups are used as fund-raising objects by Western missions, but the funds often are eaten up by secondary programs. Much of the money being raised for evangelism today is being used largely to maintain and extend the presence of unwanted Western missionary staff.

Time to Fund the Critical Needs

As Christian leaders, the key question is simple: Are we going to continue placing the priority on sending our own people abroad, or are we going to fund the authentic needs of the hour? The eternal destiny of millions of souls depends on how we choose to answer that single question.

By definition the authentic needs in any given time and place will almost always be the critical ones — the ones that deserve priority in our funding, prayer and involvement.

We must pray for discernment to separate our plans from His. Whose program is paramount — the one *we* work out, or the one the Holy Spirit defines? Whose agenda will rule — God's or man's?

Many factors come into play in deciding how best to fund the truly critical needs.

First, we must learn how to deal with the urgent. There is an urgency in missions that must be understood and moved upon — regardless of how painful it is to us. That is why missionaries must stay detached from this world and remain free to respond as God directs.

Many gospel-preaching opportunities are tied to temporary current events. Depressions, famines, wars and other circumstances cause relocations of people groups and brief openings for the gospel. The situation is often volatile and unstable, providing a brief ray of light that may disappear as quickly as it comes.

On the other hand, we need to keep a balance. The urgency of disaster, famine and war can also distort our perspective. Are we so caught up with the physical and worldly needs of the mission field that we forget the spiritual? In recent years the majority of Western missions —

especially those sent from older, established churches — have been so aware of the physical needs that they almost have missed the spiritual.

Second, we must be sensitive to open doors. The freedom to preach the gospel is often quite.fragile. So the truly mission-minded person must be sensitive to changing opportunity — ready to redeem the time for "the days are evil" (Eph. 5:16).

According to Peter Deyneka Jr., his father — the man who founded the Slavic Gospel Association — used to speak fondly of a brief time during World War II when the Soviet Union allowed Bibles to be imported freely. It happened only once in Brother Deyneka's lifetime, but it was a brief open door. At the time, the Christians in the free world did not respond, and soon the door slammed shut again. Now, as these words are being written, the door is opening again. This time Christians around the world appear to be responding and sending the Word of God to Russia.

New opportunities and strategies are always opening on some mission fields while doors are closing on others. Effective evangelism and church planting require mission boards to respond to immediate needs and opportunities. We cannot recruit and train Western personnel, hoping that political changes will come someday. Instead, we need to invest in staff and programs that will work right now.

In this sense there are no closed doors. In nearly every nation where Western missionaries are now forbidden or restricted, there are indigenous missions in desperate need of support. And there are ways to get funds and supplies through even the tightest borders.

Third, we must learn to respect the sovereign working of God. There are mysterious movings of the Holy Spirit known only to God that cause certain people to be more open to Christian witness at particular times. We do not have to understand this phenomenon to move with it.

When God pours out His Spirit, be it through indigenous missions or in any other way, we need to be sensitive and follow. The mind-set that dares to say we will only move with God if He follows our bylaws, constitution or "the way we've always done it" is not just a mistake in strategy — it is sinful rebellion against the Lord.

That traditions or nationalism is allowed to prevent us from supporting a move of the Holy Spirit should be openly exposed and rejected by sensitive leaders.

Finally, there is the matter of personality and calling. At times we find that God in His sovereignty has raised up an individual whose personality and ministry style are especially effective in reaching a certain area or people group. Again, it is important that we move with the Lord and provide special support as required by these individuals or gospel teams. This is also a critical need that must be funded whether or not the individual happens to be from our denomination, race or nationality.

By these definitions, a *critical need* does not always have to be an *emergency* need. But it is a need that requires someone on the field to sense the mind of the Lord and respond as He directs — even if it is not according to our man-made rules, prejudices and programs.

That's why the best and most effective missions today are almost always the ones that concentrate on funding critical needs. The ineffective, dying missions are the ones that are not responding to current opportunities. They are, in effect, enslaved to history and tradition.

Today's Surprising Critical Needs

What are the critical needs of our day?

Since every mission field is different, you cannot make stiff recommendations that apply to all situations. But it is safe to say that the critical needs in *most* pioneer situations are still the needs for basic gospel tools.

Key items are Bibles and New Testaments, or literature such as tracts and booklets. Illiterates need simple audio cassettes, flip charts and other teaching aids. Open-air meetings require public-address systems and generators, slide projectors and 16mm film projectors. Simple transportation such as bicycles, motorcycles and indigenous diesel vans are vital. Jeeps are helpful in some places.

Almost always these vitally needed gospel tools are manufactured and distributed by secular firms right on the mission field. It is rarely wise or necessary to import them since local goods cost less, the spare parts or repairs are easier to obtain, and they attract less attention.

Imported witnessing tools associate the gospel message with alien forces, sometimes former colonizers and invaders. It is far better to send funds to the field and let native missionaries purchase local equipment and supplies.

Why are such simple tools critical needs? The fundamental fact is most of the world's two billion unreached people are still living in rural villages. Although urbanization is occurring worldwide, the unevangelized remain in the most remote areas. India alone has over 500,000 villages, and most are still without a body of believers.

Most of the twelve thousand unreached people groups are in Third World nations — and among the poorest of the poor. The majority still live without running water, let alone electricity or television.

To reach these last tribes and tongues it is usually necessary to send men and women in on foot. The witnessing tools they carry must be inexpensive, portable and easy to use.

Since over one billion people in the world will be illiterate by A.D. 2000, and most of these are among the unreached,[1] even printed literature is often useless.

So the appropriate technology for use in many of these situations must by definition be both indigenous and back to basics.

But it would leave a false impression to say that all the critical needs in missions today are primitive. In many Third World countries radio and television are state-of-the-art mass media.

In some situations there is an urgent need for video cassettes, full-color posters, sophisticated advertising and carefully prepared tracts — especially in large cities and on university campuses.

Notes

[1]Unpublished study paper by David B. Barrett, *Global Statistics Summary* (Manila, Philippines: Lausanne II Congress on World Evangelization Statistical Task Force, July 11-20, 1989).

———————21 ———————

Listen to Indigenous
Church Leaders

I n order to understand the critical needs on a mission field, it is important to listen to the leaders of indigenous missions. Before we fund programs, we need to find out from them what tools and technologies the Holy Spirit is currently using in their land.

This requires humility and sensitivity, virtues often in short supply when Western missions launch into the field thinking that they already have all the answers.

Occidental solutions, it seems, are more and more high-tech. Too often Western plans for world evangelization are simply too complicated to succeed in the Third World. Their implementation requires infrastructures or resources that do not widely exist.

Although high-tech solutions are applicable in some situations, they are the exception rather than the rule. Any successful mission plan that succeeds in the Third World today must be based first on assisting indigenous workers. It will usually then require only the most simple local tools with a view toward the end user. In many cases that will be peasants and villagers who lack education — and sometimes electricity.

The Illusion of Television

Perhaps no better example of Western miscalculation on the mission field is the current attempts to export American televangelism around the world. The awesome power of this medium has done so much to capture the hearts and minds of an entire generation in America and Europe. Therefore, it is a strong temptation to missions looking for a shortcut to reach the world with the gospel of Jesus Christ.

Recently a major American televangelist managed to purchase thirteen weeks of half-hour programming time in Beijing on Central China Television. He thanked God publicly for what at first seemed to be a miracle breakthrough and proceeded to raise the $800,000 necessary to fund the project.

Regrettably, the project turned out to be less effective than anticipated. This disaster reveals the problem faced by those who insist on exporting *their* TV shows rather than humbly financing indigenous programs by local preachers.

First, the programs were censored. The Chinese government owns all the broadcasting channels and does not allow freedom of speech. In China, communist censors permitted the evangelist to sing and play only Southern gospel music in English.

Second, the programs were culturally inappropriate. By keeping the English-language lyrics and a musical idiom alien to China, the government was able to continue portraying Christianity as a foreign import. This foreign image would, of course, be true of almost every religious program produced in the West. Only one in a hundred might be culturally transferrable to an African or Asian audience.

Third, there was no way for the program to generate leads or be followed up by the local churches. As an outside organization without a network of local believers with whom to share responses, the evangelistic association was not able to contribute to the growth of the Chinese church.

Fourth, Third World television has a limited audience. Although Chinese TV is among the most advanced in the Third World, it still only effectively penetrates those parts of China which have electricity and are most modern. It reaches the educated urban dweller who has already been exposed to some form of Christian witness and rarely addresses the most needy audiences in rural, underdeveloped areas.

Fifth, Christian television from the West is mostly entertainment and therefore does not offer a strong enough gospel message. The content selected by the Chinese for showing was, of course, the most entertaining portions of the American televangelist's crusade ministry in the United States.

But even had they run the content of the preaching and teaching shows, the material would have been irrelevant to most Chinese viewers. American Christian television presents programs mostly designed to inspire believers in their daily walk with the Lord. It is rarely evangelistic in nature since it depends almost solely on the donations of Christian viewers to keep it going.

How erroneous we are when we measure ourselves by ourselves (2 Cor. 10:12) and depend on our own logic rather than wait on the Lord. If television will ever be used as an effective missionary tool, it certainly won't be in the form we know it in the West today.

But not all broadcasting is ineffective. I know that in the future television will become more of a common means of communication in Third World countries. However, at this point there is actually a need for much more radio broadcasting.

The Need for Radio Outreach

Right now radio is a perfect medium in many Third World countries. It is an older technology understood by many native evangelists. It is much cheaper both to produce and to purchase air time. It is often less censored, and often there are commercial stations available which sell time.

Far more people have radio receivers than TV sets, and you can find battery-operated radios even in remote village areas which don't have electricity.

Radio can be directed at unreached people groups more easily than television. Local dialects can be recorded in simple studios for broadcast back into specific regions and communities. Radio is a perfect medium to carry the spoken word and the "foolishness of preaching" which Paul said God has chosen as the primary method for winning lost souls.

We can daily reach millions of people with the gospel in some parts of Asia by using radio. For example, one program Gospel for Asia sponsors goes to five million people on a daily basis. The cost for the whole year is less than a penny per person. Radio is a bargain indeed.

The Power of the Spoken Word

But radio is not the only way to magnify and multiply the impact of the spoken word. Native missionaries desperately need simple public-address systems, hand-held bullhorns or military issue "half-mile" hailers. These loudspeakers turn street corners, markets and any public place into open-air gospel meetings.

Voice amplifiers can easily be mounted on bicycles and vans to make mobile sound trucks for gospel preaching. They also promote film showings, village crusades or meetings.

Gospel teams can park a vehicle or bicycle almost anywhere in the Third World and gather hundreds of people in just a few minutes with public-address systems. Even people who remain in their homes can hear the singing and gospel preaching clearly.

A missionary can multiply the personal impact of his preaching ministry by hundreds of times using portable bullhorns — and again the cost is minimal. A typical, small unit costs only a hundred dollars in Third World Asian countries such as India.

Large systems cost $400 in 1990, and gasoline-powered generators cost another $1,500 — a necessary cost when units are used in areas where no electricity is available.

Reaching Illiterates With Cassette Bibles and Tapes

Another rather recent miracle is the cassette tape. For less than one dollar each these modern evangelists are solving one of the most vexing problems facing missions today — how to reach the world's one billion illiterates.

Without cassette tapes and portable players, many nonreaders may never have a chance to hear the gospel. A classic example is the Auca Indians of Ecuador.

Massive world attention was focused on the Aucas when they killed five American missionaries in 1956 — men who had dedicated their lives to help translate the Bible into the Auca language.

Now, despite years of translation work, the Bible has still not been printed in the Auca language. The reason? Their tribe is too small for the Bible society to print a profitable edition of the Scripture. Also, most Aucas would not be able to read the Bible even if it were printed, since the tribe remains largely illiterate.

Meanwhile, Auca people continue to die without hearing the Word of God in their own language. Without the Bible to turn to, missionaries have struggled to disciple new believers and establish congregations among the various Auca villages where there is an interest in the gospel.

But now there is a solution. A technical missionary assistance ministry has produced the Auca Scriptures on cassette tape in cooperation with missionary translators. They have also provided the first of many hand-cranked cassette playback machines that operate without batteries, since the Auca villages still have no electricity. The technology that runs the cassette player operates on a spring drive similar to the kind that runs clocks and music boxes, only much more powerful.

Of course, the Scriptures have been available on records in many different languages for years. Missionaries probably will continue to use them, but the cassette tape technology is revolutionizing missions. The cassettes allow the native missionary to produce his own teaching messages and record whole books of the Bible for hundreds of playbacks.

Passing Through Political Barriers

In oppressive societies where restrictions on printing Bibles and literature are in effect, it is often possible to obtain blank cassettes and record the Scriptures on tape.

Often the results of a cassette tape are astonishing. In Guatemala a native missionary to the Rabinal Achi people left a simple gospel tape in a village. It was only the first eight chapters of Luke, but it was the "quick and powerful" Word of God.

Somehow it was copied and fell into the hands of a twelve-year-old boy. Awed by the power of the Scriptures, the enraptured child played it over and over again. He listened to it so often that he memorized every word.

But the story doesn't end there. The pastor of a struggling local mission church heard about the child and asked his parents if the boy could recite those eight chapters of Luke on Easter Sunday.

Missionaries say that until then the mission church was one of the driest around and had never seen a moving of the Holy Spirit. But that morning, as the boy retold the story of God's love using just the Bible itself, hearts melted.

Stubborn wills were broken by the love of God — and more than half the congregation came forward to make first-time confessions of faith. Many older Christians rededicated their lives to Christ. And that life-changing tape cost less than a dollar. Gospel tools don't have to be expensive and complicated to change lives and bring nations to Christ.

Thousands Find Christ Through Gospel Flip Charts

But there are other ways to reach those in the remote corners of our world, especially the most forgotten ones of all — illiterate farmers, the dying elderly, uneducated village women and children by the millions.

One of the cheapest and most effective tools that every native missionary needs is gospel flip charts. Do they really work? Let me answer by telling just one story that is typical of thousands.

"Old Man Mohan" was a notorious drunkard in his North Indian village. His alcoholic rages made him one of the most feared men in the area. When he was drunk, everyone in the village knew to avoid him. That's why the crowd around the native missionary gospel team quickly cleared a path for Mohan when he stumbled forward one day to sit down in the front row of the crowd.

Mohan was attracted by the bright poster colors on the gospel flip chart. He identified with the full-color sketches of a village man like himself. And the story intrigued him.

Mohan felt sorry for the villager pictured on the flip chart. He was in a difficult situation. He was running from a huge Bengal tiger, the kind that kills hundreds of Indians every year.

Grabbing a jungle vine, he escaped by rappelling over the side of a cliff. But then he saw below him a huge crocodile waiting — snapping his hungry jaws. He couldn't go up, and he couldn't go down. He was trapped.

As the story unfolded, two rats began gnawing at the vine. Soon the poor Hindu man would fall into the jaws of death. "Yes, that's just the way life is," thought Mohan as he recalled the hopeless doctrines of Hinduism which he had been taught since he was a little boy.

Mohan was captivated by the story and the despair it portrayed. He saw himself as that hopeless man.

The native missionaries who were narrating the story as they flipped the poster sheets explained that the tiger represented our sins, the crocodile represented our coming judgment at death, and the two rats represented time — the passing days and nights of our lives.

Was there any hope at all?

A gospel team member turned the laminated, plastic page to the closing scene. A ledge, shaped like a cross, appeared in the side of the cliff. "It represents the door of salvation provided by the Lord Jesus on Calvary," said the native missionary.

The doomed man in the story was able to climb onto the ledge and be saved. "You can do the same," explained the missionary in the Hindi language. "God has provided a ledge of safety for your escape from the wages of sin.

"All you need to do," said the missionary, "is step out by faith and climb onto that ledge."

Tears came to the eyes of Mohan. The gospel flip chart told the story of salvation in a modern parable that he could understand. In front of the crowd, he prayed with the native missionaries, giving the control of his life over to the Lord Jesus.

Mohan's story is repeated many times on the streets and in the villages of Third World nations where over one billion people still cannot read. In India alone there are nearly 300 million illiterates.[1]

Without wordless poster charts like these, it is hard for them to visualize the stories and truths of the Bible. That's why gospel flip charts are such a critical tool. They are light and easy to carry by bicycle or on foot. The native missionary simply rolls up the chart and carries it slung over his or her back. Neither batteries nor electricity is needed, and gospel flip charts cost little — usually less than $15 each to produce in large quantities. During the life of a flip chart, which can last for years, thousands of people can receive the gospel.

'Four Laws' on Flip Charts in Thailand

One native missionary in Thailand, Boonling Tong-Ngae, says he has seen more than ten thousand people pray the sinner's prayer after witnessing a gospel flip chart adaptation of the famous "Four Spiritual Laws" (Campus Crusade for Christ).

Boonling gathers children and elderly villagers around him as many as sixteen times a day to go over his beautiful but well-worn flip charts. He dialogues with the audience as he flips the pages, answering the questions Buddhists ask about Jesus.

At the invitation, it is not uncommon for three to four villagers to pray out loud and receive Christ while their neighbors watch with fascination and growing interest.

Large poster sheets are printed on tear-resistant paper in full color. Then they are laminated in plastic and bound in metal ring binders which allow them to be flipped easily during presentations.

Most native missionaries need three or four different flip charts in their inventory. Dollar for dollar, they find them a wonderful investment in souls.

Jesus Films Reach Millions

However, when preaching the good news of Jesus Christ to crowds, projectors and films rank at the top of the list.

There is a village in India — one of thousands like it — where most of the people can't read, no one has a TV, and there was not a single believer until recently.

Human existence was a cycle of suffering. People were born, plowed their fields, prepared and ate their food, and reproduced themselves. This cycle went on unbroken year after year until death came and, according to Hinduism, the process began all over again.

But all that changed because everyone in this village went to a movie, and that movie brought many people freedom and a new way of life.

Cinema is by far the most popular form of entertainment in India. Village people will walk miles to see a film. In fact, India has the largest movie industry in the world. Bombay produces many times more feature films each year than Hollywood.

So one day when a van drove up to the village and strung a huge sheet between two coconut trees, everyone was intrigued. By the time the portable generator was cranked up that night, people from miles around had gathered to watch.

What they saw was not a thirty-minute educational film. They did not watch a story set in an American town with the words in English or dubbed in their language.

They sat captivated throughout a dramatic, feature-length, Indian-made major studio picture called "Man of Mercy." The 35mm film would have cost millions of dollars to produce in the West.

It had Indian actors and was filmed on location in the Indian country-side, and the characters spoke the local dialect. It told the overpowering story of a man named Jesus who lived, died and rose again for their sins.

Was this film effective?

One of the Indian native missionaries tells of the reaction. "The crowd of two thousand was fascinated by Jesus' personality, the miracles He performed and the compassion He expressed.

"They cheered when He drove the moneychangers from the temple. They wept when He was beaten. When He was crucified, I heard cries of anguish. And when He arose from the dead, the audience applauded, cheered and whistled.

"With Asiatic features, wearing similar clothes, drawing water from a well and walking the dusty paths as they do, the One who 'had no place to lay His head' was instantly loved by these villagers. They could identify with Him. He was not seen as a 'white man's God' but as one of their own."

As a result of that one film showing, there is now a church of eighty-five baptized believers in that village. In fact, in the first year this film was used in India, forty new churches were formed in similar villages where there had been no previous church.

Although this film was originally produced by a Hindu, God is using it — and other similar films — to reach millions for Christ. Hundreds of copies have been made for use by native missionary teams in India and other South Asian countries.

Prints cost about $1,400 each and can be shown about 400 times before wearing out. Since the average audience is 1,500, that means each film presents the gospel to about 600,000 people at less than one-fourth cent per person!

Unlike Westerners, natives in many fields are not exposed to thousands of other media impressions, and for weeks to come they ponder and relive the dramatic messages of these Jesus films.

Films and even old-fashioned filmstrips and slides are still powerful teaching tools that can make a life-changing difference in the lives of millions. Although the video revolution has overwhelmed the West, these earlier methods of communication are still state-of-the-art in most Third World countries.

The costs are remarkably low. In India, for example, a 16mm projector in 1990 cost only $1,100, a filmstrip projector around $290, a portable generator $1,500. It is possible to outfit a film van with a complete projector, screen and sound system for $14,250. To create a similar unit in the West would probably take $50,000.

These relatively small investments in equipment can result in millions hearing the gospel — and in a face-to-face way that effectively enables native evangelists to lead people to Christ and start local churches.

Notes
[1] *A Portrait of India* (Madras, India: Church Growth Research Center, 1989), p. 11.

22

Basic Tools
Are Necessary

It may be romantic for us to picture Jesus and His disciples walking from village to village in Galilee to preach the gospel, but the reality of their journeys, like the reality of native evangelists who carry on the ministry today, is far from romantic.

Travel in many mission fields is hot, dirty, sometimes dangerous and always woefully slow.

Yet there are thousands of such gospel messengers who will walk miles under the scorching sun as Jesus did to reach yet another forgotten village with the message of God's love. In Africa, Latin America and Asia, pioneer work can require an awesome effort to reach even one new village a day.

Until recently, Nilambar (an Indian native missionary) rose every Sunday before dawn and walked nearly eleven miles to conduct morning services for the six families he had led to Christ in one village. After preaching, teaching and visiting in their homes, he walked back over the same eleven miles to a tiny room he uses as his home base. During the week he walked similar distances to take the gospel to other preaching points in his assigned district.

But he never complained about the lonely hours or the dangerous treks through the night. Suffering for the gospel was, and still is, a privilege for Nilambar. Born and raised in a staunch Hindu family, he is a Christian convert who has paid a heavy price to become a native missionary. He was disowned by his family and cast out of his home village — losing security, status and any future he once had in this world. He is still hated and persecuted by his family and friends.

Because of his proven faithfulness, dedication and fruit-bearing ministry, Nilambar was recently chosen to receive a bicycle to help in his outreach ministry. Overnight his effectiveness increased almost 300 percent. With the added speed of his new bike, he is able to reach two or three villages each day instead of only one.

When Asians come to the West, they are surprised to discover that bikes are used mostly as children's toys or for sports and recreation. Asian bikes are heavy-duty, workhorse vehicles built for a long life of service on some of the roughest roads and trails in the world.

A missionary on foot is greatly limited in what he can carry. But a heavy-duty bicycle allows him to carry up to 150 pounds of equipment and supplies: tracts, books, a megaphone and even projectors.

With a bike, a native missionary extends his reach by at least twenty miles in every direction, and that makes a huge difference in the number of villages that can be reached. This is especially true in the more densely populated areas. Some native missionaries can count up to three hundred villages within a day's biking distance of their home base.

In China, Bangladesh, India, Pakistan and Vietnam, the bicycle is the primary method of transportation, both for people and commercial deliveries. The same is true for many African and some European nations. Even in some of the Latin American countries the bike remains the single most important method of transportation for soul-winning evangelists.

How Smoking a Gospel Tract Brought Salvation

Satish Sahu had never seen a tract or heard the story of God's love. He was a Hindu acolyte to the demon idols of a little village near Simdega, Bihar State, in North India.

One night all that changed when a native missionary gave him his first gospel tract. Like tens of millions around him, he had never before received the Word of God in any form.

In order to find peace and forgiveness of sin, each year he would travel hundreds of miles to scoop water from the River Ganges. Then he would carry some back, traveling from one idol shrine to another with the village priest. There they would anoint the filthy stone idols, bowing before the images of demons.

Satish was enraged when he first saw the native missionary preaching in his all-Hindu village. Breaking up the street meeting, he argued that Hinduism had 333 million gods and goddesses to bring salvation — not just one God like the Christians.

Taking the gospel tract home, he began tearing the pages out to roll opium cigarettes in them. But that night he could not sleep. The Holy Spirit began to deal with him about the contents of the tract.

In the darkness he lit a candle and read some of the pages he had torn apart. Then he found the words that changed his life: "The blood of Christ cleanses us from all sin."

The next morning Satish went to the quarters of the native missionary with a broken and repentant heart. After some hours of questioning, he committed his life to Christ.

"I felt a great burden removed from my back," testifies Satish today. He then started riding his bike thirty-five miles to fellowship with the nearest Christians. He grew rapidly in the Lord because he was very soon able to obtain his own copy of the Bible, a rare book in that part of the world.

Satish and his family were bitterly persecuted for his new faith. His own father, who had been a Hindu priest for twenty-two years, was beaten by fanatics for allowing his son to become a Christian. The whole village turned on them. But eventually Satish led his father and brother to Christ. Soon many others in the village listened to the witness of Satish and turned from idols as well.

Today Satish pastors a growing church among the Birhor tribal people and still regularly preaches to Hindus in the markets. All this because of the power of a simple gospel tract.

There are millions of stories like this one — testimonies of people whose lives have been changed by a simple gospel tract. In Third World nations such as India, gospel tracts are not thrown away on the streets as they are in the West.

The printed word is treasured. Tracts are read and reread, passed from hand to hand until they wear out. Asians and Africans who can read are hungry for books, pamphlets and tracts of all kinds.

Even simple gospel tracts in some places can have the power of a book or magazine in the United States or Canada. For $50 it is still possible to print as many as ten thousand of these tracts.

Our mailboxes in the West are jammed with Christian magazines, newspapers and appeals for funds, but on the mission fields millions have not yet seen their first gospel tract. Some Christians will receive three or four different devotional guides a month while two billion have yet to receive a copy of John 3:16.

It is possible to change this pattern if we will insist on changing our priorities in printing and distributing Christian literature.

I would like to propose a special literature tithe. Everyone who buys a book or Bible in the West would tithe 10 percent of the purchase price for overseas gospel literature. Christian bookstores and catalog houses might agree to collect it at the time of purchase. It could be part of their ministry to the lost souls still without their first-ever gospel tract. And, of course, we as purchasers of Christian literature could collect our own tithe and contribute it quarterly for native Christian literature.

Such a "self-tax" on the billion-dollar Christian book and gift business in the United States could produce $80 million a year — a wonderful step toward meeting the needs for gospel literature in the Third World.

The Word of God Still the Number-one Need

Although few realize it, by the year 2000 we could face a real crisis in Bible printing and distribution. That is unless Christians in the affluent West renew their commitment to sharing the Word of God. The open doors for Bible distribution in Soviet Asia and China are immense, and the need for Bibles and Scripture portions could soon run into billions of dollars.

The worldwide Bible shortage produces incredible stories of people who hand-copy the Bible page by page. Others have been known to photograph it, photocopy it and beg for it.

Some believers have cried when they received their first Bible, and kissed it joyfully. That's how precious the Word of God is to those who have not had it. Often Bibles are chained to the pulpits in churches so they won't be stolen.

The true story of A. Stephen is absolutely astonishing. Soon after he found Jesus, someone gave him a Bible; but it was printed in the language of the next state, so he couldn't understand a word.

But he was so hungry to read anything about the living God that he spent the next six months teaching himself the new language so he could read the wonderful words of life. That's how precious the Word of God is in India, a land where hundreds of millions of people still have never even seen a copy of the Bible.

Asia is a vast continent starved for the Word of God. Most of the world's twelve thousand unreached people groups are located there, almost all without the Bible translated into their mother tongues. Imagine — two billion people without the Bible, a gospel of John, a church or Christ!

By printing Bibles 100,000 copies at a time, in some countries it is possible to get especially low prices. In India, for example, Bibles can be produced for around $3. When we compare this to the study Bibles and special editions that cost $40 to $150 in the West, it would appear that we should alter our priorities.

Bible counters in religious bookstores of the United States are rich with the smell of beautiful leather Bibles. Ironically, most of these luxury Bibles are printed on India paper, bound with Australian cowhide, manufactured in England, financed by Dutch banks and imported to the United States. Bookshelves in many homes in the West are lined with numerous versions of the Bible, while so many millions overseas are starving for a single copy of the Word of God.

This is dangerous spiritual gluttony. Where are the Christian leaders, pastors and mission advocates who will have the courage to stand up and hold the Western church accountable for hoarding the wonderful words of life?

Funding the Critical Needs

Our mission dollars will go further and make a New Testament impact if we concentrate on supporting critically needed evangelism rather than putting such a large percentage of funds into pre-evangelism witness programs. Such a strategy will produce immediate, measurable results in terms of more evangelism, numbers of converts and numbers of churches planted.

Millions are not hearing the plan of salvation clearly articulated because native missionaries and gospel teams lack simple witnessing tools. If affluent Christians in the West would sacrifice to supply these tools, completing the task of world evangelism could be rapidly accelerated.

Pastors, missions committee chairpersons, missions leaders and donors in the West can insist on these changes in missions policy. And unless leadership redirects funds to these critical needs, the Great Commission may not be completed in our lifetime.

23

Send Authentic
Missionaries

Missions is much more than fulfilling the critical needs for soul-winning tools on the mission field. It is being ready to obey, as the church in Antioch did, when the Lord says, "Separate me Barnabas and Saul for the work whereunto I have called them" (Acts 13:2).

Ultimately, this is the most critical part of the missionary enterprise: identifying and sending out His servants.

God's Man for the Hmong of Dallas

I didn't really know what to expect that Sunday afternoon in Dallas. For months Bob Winfield had been inviting us to come and challenge his tiny refugee congregation of Hmongs in Dallas. I had heard about Bob. He was a Dallas-based missionary pastor to several thousand Laotian immigrants. They had been flown to northern Texas from Southeast Asia by the U.S. government at the end of the Vietnam War.

I'd never met Bob personally, and quite frankly my flesh simply didn't want to go and preach to these strange people. As I prayed about it, the Lord seemed to say go. I'm glad I obeyed, because I learned a valuable lesson that day.

When American forces pulled out of Southeast Asia, several hundred thousand of the primitive Hmongs fled across the Mekong River to refugee camps in northeast Thailand. Many were then evacuated, mostly to the United States. They were processed along with other Southeast Asian refugees — boat people from South Vietnam and Khmers from the land war in Cambodia.

Many came to refugee camps barefoot, illiterate and totally unable to cope with the destruction of their homes and way of life. What little the surviving men knew about modern technology was related to weapon systems and small arms. Moreover, most of the refugees were widows and children. At first none could use a telephone, toilet, electric range or automobile — let alone speak English or hold a job.

A Church Responds to the Fall of Saigon

Meanwhile, when Saigon fell, Bob and some friends from his church in Dallas prayed and decided the Lord would have them sponsor some Vietnamese refugees. They had never heard of the Hmong, so when they met these tribal people for the first time, nothing was quite like what they expected it to be.

In their homeland, these refugees had been migratory mountaineers. They clung to the barren hillsides of north central Laos and had subsisted for centuries by slash-and-burn farming. For the last two to three years they had lived in concentration camps. Then they landed at the Dallas-Fort Worth airport.

Vietnam vets recognized they were from Southeast Asia and tried to greet them in broken Vietnamese and "G.I. Thai." But the Hmong couldn't explain that they weren't Vietnamese. They were taken by Christian volunteers to tiny apartments on the wrong side of the tracks. Well-meaning Christians loaded up their pantries with Mexican rice and beans.

Suddenly they found themselves settled in strange cities and towns under a huge Texas sky. There was not a mountain in sight. This was the end of the line, a new home where they couldn't speak the language or use any of their natural skills to survive.

Religiously, they were animists. They worshipped spirits in rocks, trees, streams and land formations. Their religion consisted mostly of casting spells, using good-luck charms and sacrificing chickens to malevolent spirits. All this was a bit difficult for their Southern Baptist sponsors to comprehend.

A Nobody for Jesus

Nothing could have prepared me for what I found when we arrived for their worship service.

Bob, a white-skinned Texan, was dressed in a ceremonial wraparound sarong skirt like the other Hmong males. He was sitting on the floor cross-legged like the others. He was speaking Hmong with the new believers and eating with his fingers. Before him on the plate was their foul-smelling Sunday feast of sticky rice, dried fish, hot peppers in fish sauce and fermented coleslaw.

If Bob felt strange, it didn't show. He genuinely seemed to enjoy eating this ethnic treat with his congregation, who considered the Sunday meal their gourmet highlight of the week.

Most of all, I could see the love of Jesus beaming from Bob's eyes. Here was a husky Texan holding hands with a Hmong man, as is their custom, and sharing with them at their level.

Bob was giving up his culture, his customs, his food, his language and his time to reach out to a people who were nobodies by Texas standards.

Others had welcomed the Hmong once or twice at the beginning with the traditional down-home hospitality for which Texas is so famous: barbeque beef, square dancing, rope twirling. Some had even attempted evangelism by sharing the "Four Spiritual Laws" in English using an overhead projector.

Somebody obtained Laotian Bibles, not realizing that although the Hmong came from Laos, they did not read Laotian.

The Key to the Hmong Heart

The American witnesses meant well. They tried their best. But the confused Hmong smiled politely on the outside while crying on the inside. They sensed that the Americans were trying in their own way to show some concern, but they needed someone who would love them on their terms and become one with them first. Only then could they hear the message of this American Jesus.

In other words, they needed a missionary who would become a nobody like them for Jesus' sake. Someone had to take the time to understand the Hmong. Unless that someone would abandon his or her culture and identify with them, they were never going to be able to understand the gospel.

Perhaps their children might make the transition into American society, but they needed someone to reach out to them right now.

Bob decided he would be that man for the Hmong of Dallas. He identified as fully as he could, learning their language and adopting their ways.

In the end he not only became their pastor, but a social worker, friend, English teacher and evangelist. Today there is a tiny Hmong church in Dallas, and many Hmong will be in heaven because Bob did what it always takes to be an effective missionary. He died to self.

One of the greatest hindrances to successful missionary work is selfish ambition. Whenever a person tries to build a kingdom for himself in this world — to protect his way of life, culture or doctrine — he is automatically disqualified from building the kingdom of God.

Jesus said we cannot follow Him unless we deny ourselves, take up the cross and daily follow after Him. This is what authentic missionary work is all about. It is as near as one gets to the definition of what it means to be a true missionary.

While current political, economic and social barriers make it imperative for us to shift our support to a more balanced indigenous missions policy, this is only one part of the reformation needed in world missions today.

As I watched Bob move among those Hmong people that Sunday in Dallas, I realized that by exercising that same Christlike spirit in Laos or India or Afghanistan, he would be equally successful in evangelism and church planting there. He had the Spirit of Christ, which any missionary needs to touch the hearts of people for God.

That doesn't mean an indigenous missionary team isn't still the best strategy on most fields today. However, it does mean that no missionary, native or foreign, can follow the call to missions unless he is willing to let that call possess his total person.

The Lord Jesus, the apostle Paul and every successful missionary model since them have had this in common. They emptied themselves of ego and identified fully with those they were sent to reach.

As Paul said, the way of the cross is always "not I, but Christ" (Gal. 2:20).

The Big Question Is Not Race or Nationality

When it comes to sending out missionaries, the supreme issue is really not how we will determine our current staffing policies concerning native missionaries. Far more important is whether or not the missionary candidate has truly received a call from God and is responding to it.

In other words, whom are we sending out? Are we commissioning the real thing or a counterfeit? Is this missionary called to the work — and gifted by God supernaturally for service?

Just going across the street or across the ocean does not make a person a missionary. Only God can do that. At best, the sending church or mission board must determine whether God has sovereignly set aside a person for missionary service.

Hence, the proper commissioning procedure waits on the Holy Spirit to set aside certain individuals for missionary service. That's why the Antioch believers prayed and fasted before setting aside the first missionaries; they waited for the Lord to guide them.

Why William Carey Best Exemplifies True Missionary Spirit

William Carey is often called the father of modern missions. It is a well-earned epitaph. He demonstrated an authentic missionary life-style. He had *both* the calling and the gifts of the Holy Spirit that characterize a genuine envoy of the Lord.

That doesn't mean that even the best missionary won't make mistakes. William Carey at times miscalculated or misjudged situations, pursuing practices and policies that are debatable today. Yet, as David testified in another age, God intervened and "saved him out of all his troubles" as promised in Psalm 34:6.

He manifested the missionary motivational gifts of Ephesians 4:11. Carey was already a proven apostle, evangelist and prophet before he went to India. He arrived there with a New Testament definition of his work already in mind. His goal, he said, was "to build an indigenous church 'by means of native preachers.' "[1] His translation and educational efforts were simply necessary steps toward the goal, never an end in themselves.

Carey was uncompromising in his obedience to the missionary call. In fact, when asked to reveal the secret of his success, he replied simply, "I can plod. I can persevere in any definite pursuit. To this I owe everything."[2] He was the first to go to North India on a one-way ticket, never returning to England even for a furlough during his forty years of service. He lived and died at the place of his calling, the mouth of the mighty Ganges River.

The thought of security, retirement, safety or his own future was never an issue. For the sake of India's lost millions, Carey gave up everything. He lived and died in poverty, never considering opportunities to enrich himself from the treasures of the East India Company trade that flourished around him.

In England Carey fought a church and theological establishment that ridiculed his qualifications, doctrines and basic understanding of the Great Commission. Once on the field, Carey faced a pioneer situation that is unimaginable to most of us today.

Misunderstood by fellow Christians and eventually betrayed by the board which sent him to Calcutta, he fought nearly his whole life against a solid wall of hostility. Hated by the white traders of the British East India Company, he discovered that he was shunned in Calcutta by both the British colonialists and the Hindus he had come to reach.

His first wife, Dorothy, refused to support Carey in his vision of overseas missionary work. She would not join him in the mission until he was practically on board ship for India. Once in India, she continued to resist and finally became "wholly deranged" after the tragic death of their five-year-old son in 1794.[3] Carey cared for his sickly children and mentally ill wife for thirteen more years, unwilling to return to England or to slow down with his witnessing and translation work.

When the promised support from Christians in London failed to arrive, he worked in an indigo mill to support himself and refused to consider returning home. He faced spiritual and other barriers that can only be compared to what believers today might face in anti-Christian lands such as China, Libya, Cuba or North Korea. Besides this, he had no missionary role model or teacher to disciple him, only the Bible to guide him in his new work.

The Serampore Covenant

Despite the lack of a senior missionary mentor, Carey discovered and wrote out eleven amazing principles that have since become known as the Serampore Covenant. He required all his staff to affirm publicly the terms of the covenant three times a year:

To set an infinite value on the souls of men.

To acquaint ourselves with the snares which hold the minds of the people in bondage.

To abstain from whatever deepens India's prejudice against the gospel.

To watch for every chance of doing the people good.

To preach Christ crucified as the grand means of conversion.

To esteem and treat Indians always as our equals.

To guard and build up the flock that has been gathered.

To cultivate their spiritual gifts, ever pressing upon them their missionary obligation, since only Indians can win India for Christ.

To labor unceasingly in biblical translation.

To be instant in the nurture of personal religion.

To give ourselves without reserve to the cause, not counting even the clothes that we wear as our own.[4]

In these principles, Carey showed that he had grasped the essentials of authentic missionary work: love and respect for the people, a commitment to winning souls and making disciples, a willingness to sacrifice, a commitment to indigenous missionaries and a dedication to consistent personal holiness. The fruit of Carey's ministry is amazing by today's standards.

Most of all, Carey won many to Christ and established pioneer congregations in numerous unreached people groups — including all the major ethnic groups of the Ganges River Valley.

Today the same biblical principles and life-style which he embraced are being reapplied by hundreds of indigenous missionary societies in India and throughout the Third World.

The principles of successful missionary work were taught by Jesus and the apostles from the beginning. The first challenge facing any missions committee, pastor or sending church today is finding true missionaries like Carey who are living and working according to the New Testament pattern. The second challenge is to reform our sending policies and transfer critical assistance to these brethren so that they can continue to move into new territories for the Lord.

_____

Notes

[1]Ruth A. Tucker, *From Jerusalem to Irian Jaya* (Grand Rapids, Mich.: Zondervan Publishing House, 1983), p. 121.

[2]Mary Drewery, *William Carey: A Biography* (Grand Rapids, Mich.: Zondervan Publishing House, 1979), p. 25.

[3]Tucker, *From Jerusalem to Irian Jaya*, p. 117.

[4]Unpublished study paper by Abraham Philip, *Third World Missions: Interfacing With Western Missions* (Manila, Philippines: Lausanne II Congress on World Evangelization, July 1989), pp. 2-3.

24

How to Locate
Authentic Missionaries

Thousands of native missionaries are following in the footsteps of Carey. As a result, an average of one thousand new churches are being formed every day worldwide. In some nations, such as the Philippines, a new church is formed every eight hours. By A.D. 2000 Filipino church planters are expecting to see fifty thousand new congregations planted as part of a ten-year national strategy.[1]

A spokesman for the U.S. Center for World Mission in Pasadena, California, has estimated that in China twenty-four thousand to twenty-eight thousand people a day are coming to Christ despite the oppression following the Tiananmen Square massacre in June 1989.

Similar astonishing growth is occurring through indigenous movements today in Brazil, India, Korea, Nigeria, Thailand and Indonesia — nations where Western missionaries are banned or extremely ineffective.

Pius Wakatama, author of *Independence for the Third World Church*, comments on these changes taking place in Africa: "It is time to realize that, although the Western missionary movement has had a glorious past in Africa and has accomplished much, we have reached the end of an era and are seeing the dawn of a new one. There is much Africans can learn from the experiences of their Western missionary forebears. However, our situation is drastically different from the days of the pioneer missionaries, and we cannot just ape what they did. We need to listen to what God is telling us in our own age and in our own situation."[2]

Times are different, and the main work of the harvest is now in the hands of indigenous workers. But our missionary sending and funding policies have been slow to catch up with what has happened on the field.

The frontline work of missions today has already shifted into the hands of indigenous mission boards. Missiologist Larry Pate, author of *From Every People*, reports that indigenous missions are now growing five times faster than traditional missions — 13.4 percent annually or 248 percent during the last decade.[3]

Even though Pate does not acknowledge hundreds of thousands of independent missionaries, he still predicts that the number of indigenous missionaries will surpass foreign missionaries by 1998.

By the year 2000 non-Western missionaries will comprise 54.5 percent of the total missionary force, or over 162,000 workers.[4]

These estimates are based on the assumption that present trends will continue. But many native missionary leaders believe the tempo of change will quicken. This will mean even *more* natives offering themselves for service in the coming decade.

David Cho, chairman of the Third World Missions Association, is calling for one million native missionaries to volunteer by the turn of the century. Even if Cho reaches only half his goal, that would mean 500,000 native missionaries on the field by A.D. 2000.

Thus, while Western mission societies struggle to recruit and train hundreds of staff, native missionaries by the thousands are waiting for sponsors to send them into the fields.

So reports of a missionary staff shortage are actually inaccurate. Except for some neglected Muslim fields and in some Marxist-controlled regions, there are large numbers of native Christians who are ready to be challenged and sent forth into the harvest.

Challenge Two: Change Our Sending Policies

Sadly, missions policies in most of our evangelical churches are twenty to fifty years behind the reality on the mission fields today. All too often our missions programs are still prisoners of outdated policies based on the realities of the harvest fields just after World War II.

• Many of the oldest and most important "missions churches" in the United States and Canada have adopted missions policies that limit their ability to fund effective, New Testament missionaries. In many cases these old rules and traditions are being applied in a way that was never intended by their authors. Sometimes these very rules are now hindering rather than fulfilling the Great Commission.

• Some mission agencies and important "missions churches" have adopted bylaws that actually forbid them from supporting indigenous missions. Whatever the logic was for the policy when it was adopted forty or fifty years ago, it is now time to amend the constitution.

• Others have adopted rules that forbid missionary support going to anyone other than those of their particular denomination or theological conviction. Thus, when an effective indigenous missionary movement emerges that is not controlled by their denominational leadership, the rules forbid support, no matter how excellent the ministry may be.

It is important to note that this aid is not denied to indigenous missions because of a conflict over *essential doctrines*. Aid is almost always denied because of a particular sectarian emphasis, slant or "spin" on Bible teaching that disagrees with that of the sending church.

We must realize that Jesus has not sent us into the harvest field to plant Baptist, Congregational, Episcopal, Pentecostal or Reformed churches. Most of these Western labels don't even apply accurately on the mission field. (Indigenous movements are more likely to be loosely defined in terms of our Western doctrinal divisions.)

• Finally, some well-meaning churches have long-standing commitments to certain mission fields, mission agencies and individuals. Often these loyalties are to people and organizations who have completed their pioneer work and are no longer on the front lines of world evangelism. In these cases also, painful decisions must be made to step out and obey the Holy Spirit — responding to the greater needs of pioneer native missionaries who are now working with unreached people groups on the frontiers.

Because the change to an indigenous policy is logical, righteous and wise on paper doesn't mean it is easy to make when the time comes to vote for a change in the budget. Old connections, relationships and networks are hard to sacrifice, but is God asking us to make new ones in light of current conditions?

Human pride is hurt when asked to give up the feeling of direct control that old-fashioned, traditional missionary structures have provided over the years. But were these desires to dominate others of the Lord in the first place?

Time for Repentance and Revival

In order to shift our policies from a "going" mode to a "sending" mode, we need to experience repentance and a revival of our overall burden for the purpose of missions. Many churches and individuals who have lost the vision for the unreached world need to renew their basic commitment to the Great Commission and world evangelism.

A Great Commission Christian doesn't care who gets the glory or who is on the front lines. Instead, he is willing to be a "goer" or a "sender" as the Lord leads. If our hearts are in the right place, we will want to be involved in the battle wherever the Commander-in-Chief puts us. We know from Acts 1:8 that it takes the whole church working together to reach Jerusalem, Judea, Samaria and the uttermost parts of the earth.

Ultimately, it will take prayer and re-education for us to be involved in the lives of indigenous missionaries. They are rarely able to travel to the West to inspire us as Western missionaries do from the older, colonial-style missions. It takes a little more work to communicate with indigenous missionaries, understand them and learn about their needs.

Becoming a partner with indigenous missions requires more faith in God and a willingness to trust in our brothers and sisters in the Third World. This is a challenge to our comfortable prejudices and notions about other nationalities and people.

Notes

[1]Unpublished study paper by David B. Barrett, *Global Statistics Summary* (Manila, Philippines: Lausanne II Congress on World Evangelization Statistical Task Force, July 11-20, 1989).

[2]Article by Pius Wakatama, "The Role of Africans in the Third World Mission of the Church," *Evangelical Missions Quarterly* (Wheaton, Ill.: Evangelical Missions Information Service, April 1990), p. 130.

[3]Larry D. Pate, *From Every People* (Monrovia, Calif.: MARC Publications, 1989), p. 45.

[4]*Ibid.*, p. 51.

Turning the Tide

Western mission agencies and churches are facing a painful challenge in the 1990s and beyond. We must base our missions policies on supporting whoever is doing the work of the gospel — not on who is going overseas from our circle of friends.

• We must stop talking about "our" plans and start promoting "their" plans.

• We must take money from "our" budgets and give it to "their" budgets.

• We must stop planning to send "our" people and decide we're going to send "their" people.

• We must find new ways to be informed and involved about world missions emotionally, mentally and spiritually without actually depending on having "our" people resident on the foreign fields.

• We must pray and work to amend bylaws and constitutions that chain us to colonial missions policies and practices. Any program or policy that doesn't put the priority on funding native missionaries and programs needs to re-evaluated. Prejudice and nationalism must not be allowed to determine church or missions policy.

Yes, missions have entered a new and exciting era, but they still depend on the presence of godly missionaries whom God has called and prepared to labor in His harvest field. And today they are far more likely to have black, brown or yellow skin.

The challenge of Romans 10:13-15 still speaks to us, demanding that we stay invested in this people process till Christ returns. Mass media and other modern technologies are important, but they cannot replace the frontline missionary church planter. Missionaries are still the foot soldiers in the army of the Lord.

The True Story of Thomas Mathew

Thousands of native missionaries today are exhibiting the authentic life-styles still demanded to win souls and plant churches. Yet most live their whole ministries without the support they need to reach the lost on their field.

Thomas Mathew, a pioneer missionary to Rajasthan, is typical. He grew up in a nominally Christian home in Kerala, the most Christianized state in South India.

As a teenager he was miraculously saved from drowning in a swimming accident. Though never particularly missions-minded before that day, the closeness of death had a profound effect on his adolescent mind. Realizing God must have saved his life for a purpose, he dedicated himself to the most radical kind of service he could imagine — becoming a missionary in North India.

Ministry in North India is an enormous sacrifice for believers in the South. They must give up the normal comforts they have grown up with, moving from lush jungles to scorching-hot plains, from beautiful coasts and rain forests to a world of dust and deserts.

Food, dress, language, culture and religion change. Surrounded by a comfortable, relatively Christian atmosphere in the South, they go to areas where Hindus, Sikhs and Muslims have traditionally resisted Christ for centuries.

But, to an Indian, the most painful sacrifice of all is giving up career and family ties with all the security they promise.

For Thomas the decision to serve Christ was viewed as absolutely insane by most of his family and friends. It meant giving up a fine future as an engineer.

A professor from his school was so distraught at hearing of his decision that he visited the family in their home, begging his parents to forbid Thomas from going.

But his parents had dedicated him to the Lord before he was born and could not stand in the way of their son's apparently suicidal desire to start a ministry in Rajasthan — then known as the graveyard of Christian missions in India.

So without the backing of a church, mission board or any other visible means of support, he used everything he had to go to the North.

When Thomas arrived, he had two rupees, or about ten cents, in his pocket. That was in 1962. Today he has helped plant hundreds of congregations and has a staff of 250 missionaries. He has a Bible school and evangelistic teams that range over several Indian states.

Between then and now there were many sleepless nights on the street, days without food, beatings, firebombings and the martyrdom of several who came to Christ through his ministry.

The Test of Finances

At one of the lowest points during his early ministry Thomas fell three months behind in the rent on his single room. Although the rent was only fifteen rupees (or about $1.50) a month, he was so poor he didn't have money for food, let alone the rent. Without food for days, he was slowly starving and almost discouraged enough to quit.

His angry Hindu landlord came demanding the rent of forty-five rupees ($4.50). When Thomas didn't have it, he threatened to come back the next day and throw him out.

As yet there were no Christian converts in the area. Like most pioneer missionaries, he had no one on earth to turn to for help in a hostile community which hated the presence of a missionary in their midst.

He had prayed and fasted for days. He was in such despair that all he could do was huddle under his blanket like a child and cry out to God.

The next morning he heard a loud knock at the door. Fearing the landlord, he didn't answer. But the stubborn caller wouldn't quit. Finally he got up.

"Go away!" he shouted, thinking it was the landlord. "I'm leaving today!"

"Open up," said the voice on the other side. "I have a registered letter for you."

When he opened the letter, Thomas found a postal money order for fifty rupees, or about $5. It was enough to pay the back rent and buy food for a week.

This story can be repeated thousands of times in India and almost every Third World nation. The few dollars that cannot even buy a meal in an American restaurant are enough to keep a soldier of the cross alive for days on the mission fields of the Third World.

For those who know Thomas Mathew today as one of the boldest and most courageous missionary leaders of North India, it is hard to imagine a time when he was so destitute. But this is a true story Thomas often recounts today.

There are other true stories of missionaries whose children have died for want of food and medical care; others who have slept in the street for months as homeless persons; others who go hungry and without simple gospel witnessing tools because there is no one to support them in the ministry to which God has called them.

Why Penalize Native Missionaries?

Are these foolish men and women who went out without planning? Are they lazy and shiftless? Are these missionaries without the spiritual covering of elders and mission boards?

No, these are simply devoted missionaries who have chosen to obey the Lord no matter what the cost. They are missionaries who counted the cost, knew the risks and still went out to fulfill the Great Commission on faith. In fact, it is these native missionaries who are now writing the final chapters of the book of Acts.

Should they be penalized for their trust in the Lord and simple obedience because rich Christians in the affluent nations of the world have no "easy way" to support them?

Our budgets can be changed to support indigenous mission agencies and supply the needs of native missionaries. Why don't we make these changes now?

This is the question every concerned Christian in the West should be asking. It is the question which church leaders at every level should be answering. It is already too late to wait any longer.

Positive Steps
Toward Wise Giving

The year was 1916. He looked strangely out of place among his impeccably dressed, English-looking Indian colleagues. Wearing typical Indian clothing, he sat on the platform and waited for his turn to speak.

It had been over a year since he had returned to his native land from South Africa. The past twelve months had given him a chance to observe his country. He had listened to grievances aired by the poor and downtrodden and heard brave plans for India's future from those who wanted Britain to "quit India."

He had heard enough. Now Mohandas K. Gandhi was ready to speak.

He stood and faced his audience. Most of them were India's elite, dependent upon the British to perpetuate their comfortable life-styles. Not one was prepared to hear Gandhi's bold plan of civil disobedience to free India from British rule. And certainly they were not ready for his method of attack, which was to identify with his own people instead of living above them. But this was exactly what Gandhi proceeded to tell them.

"Foreign rule would be replaced, he said, when Indian leaders begin to serve the needs of the villagers better than the British. Thus, to the keen discomfort of the educated and the well-to-do, did Gandhi begin his ministry in India."[1]

Gandhi had made a commitment to become one with his people, to stand beside them and not above them. He wore Indian-made clothing instead of British-made, and he traveled in the third-class train compartment rather than in first-class comfort.

Gandhi saw the peril into which these wealthy, educated men had fallen. They were calling for home rule, and yet all the while they had slowly become just like those they were fighting to escape. They longed to be free of colonialism but had taken on the same mannerisms of the people who were over them.

In the Third World today, some national missionary leaders are living and working just as these educated Indians were — separate from their own people. They continue to live above the life-styles of their lost countrymen, and their ability to reach out with the gospel of Jesus Christ is seriously hindered.

Many of these leaders have traveled abroad, pleading their cause to the churches in the West. Well-meaning Christians have given out of love and compassion for the lost, not knowing that sometimes these funds went to perpetuate comfortable life-styles rather than further the gospel.

As believers longing to reach the Third World's unreached, what can we do to give wisely and with discernment? The answer is not to give up supporting nationals. Instead, we must be as discerning with them as we are with any other opportunity to invest the money God has entrusted to us for the sake of His kingdom. This discernment will require asking appropriate questions and looking to God for guidance.

Being native doesn't guarantee genuineness, purity, consistency or effectiveness any more than being North American does. But when measured by appropriate standards, *if qualities of value are equal,* native missionaries generally yield a far greater harvest for the investment.

The Classroom of Experience

It is often said that failure is the best teacher. How very true this is! In our beginning days, we at Gospel for Asia often had to learn these lessons through our own mistakes.

The lessons we have learned over the years from our experiences have proven invaluable. Gospel for Asia now has a team of mature Christian men who travel full-time, meeting with and evaluating native missionary prospects. We have learned what to look for in a man or woman's character, the nature of their ministries and the fruit that results. Consequently, we can provide support with joy and confidence in the brothers and sisters we serve.

Taking the Offensive in Wise Giving

The challenge before us to give wisely and with discernment is not insurmountable. There are steps to take which will ensure accountability, trust and a great deal of satisfaction knowing that funds are being spent efficiently for the Lord's kingdom.

However, because our investment in evangelizing these countries pushes us abruptly into spiritual warfare, we simply cannot expect a 100-percent success rate. Failures and mistakes will occur. That is why we must move with the Lord's leading. Beyond all that we could ever *know*, we still need to take that step of faith. As we humble ourselves before Him, seek His guidance and move forward carefully, He will lead us to His servants who need support.

We must understand the missionary or mission board under consideration for support. Three areas need to be covered in the evaluation process: a) financial and administrative standards; b) personal life-style and character; and c) ministry fruit. (Note: the only exception in the "ministry fruit" category would be a new missionary recruit who has not yet begun his or her ministry.)

Here are questions which Gospel for Asia asks of any indigenous mission group or individual missionary seeking financial support from us. Answers to questions such as these will give greater insight into the nature and workings of the ministry being considered. Some questions will apply more to an organization than to an individual, and vice versa.

Financial and Administrative Standards

1. Is an annual audit done by a certified accountant?
2. Is the audit made available to the organization's constituency?
3. Is the ratio of spending for field ministry considerably greater

than for administration? (It should be at least 80 percent for actual ministry.)

4. Are all documents, assets and the like in the name of the organization (not an individual leader)?

5. What are the major items of expense? (If funds go primarily for properties, hospitals and schools rather than for actual field evangelism, be *extremely* cautious to check them out.)

6. Is the missionary or group receiving any financial assistance from other sources?

7. Is there a written agreement to declare all sources of income for any given project?

8. Is the group registered with the government as a charitable or nonprofit organization?

9. Are finances and financial records handled only by the leader and his relatives? (If this is the case, then you have good enough reason *not* to support him.)

10. Are the accounts jointly operated (that is, at least two people responsible for handling the funds)?

11. Are written and signed receipts kept for records of how money was spent for any given project or missionary?

12. Who makes decisions which govern the activities of the mission?

Personal Life-style and Character

1. Is the missionary involved in full-time ministry (at least eight hours a day) in an unreached area?

2. Approximately how much time does the missionary spend in personal Bible study and prayer?

3. Is the missionary working among non-Christians? (The exception would be a Bible school teacher working with missionary trainees.)

4. How long has the missionary been working on this assignment?

5. What kind of training for ministry has the missionary had?

6. Does the missionary exhibit the qualifications for service listed in 1 and 2 Timothy?

7. Is the missionary sure of a clear call that God has placed upon his or her life?

8. How does the missionary view his or her ministry? (If you sense it is more of a "job" rather than a walk of faith, beware!)

9. Is the missionary living at the level of the people he or she is serving?

10. Does the missionary work well with others, or do you hear of conflicts with his or her co-workers?

11. How long has the missionary been saved?

12. How long has the missionary been in the ministry?

13. What is the missionary's basic doctrinal position?

Questions specifically regarding native missionary leaders:

1. Are they mature in the faith, having successfully planted churches previously?

2. Are the leaders willing to meet regularly with the native missionaries under them for prayer, fellowship and sharing?

3. Do the leaders display a servant's heart, not desiring direct control over missionaries' lives?

4. Do they care for the spiritual well-being of those under them? (Leaders are responsible to see that native missionaries are qualified for service and remain so in the years following.)

5. Do they have a definite vision for the organization?

6. What standard of living do the native missionary leaders maintain?

Ministry Fruit

1. Does the missionary have a good testimony among the people?

2. Does the missionary manage his or her own household well?

3. Is he or she a model of sacrificial giving and service?

4. How much gospel literature has been distributed during the past year?

5. How many have been led to the Lord in the past year?

6. How many have been baptized in the past year?

7. How many have dedicated their lives for full-time service to the Lord in the past year?

8. How many churches were established in the past year? Give such details as name of village, population, major religion, date the church started, number of believers and place of worship.

9. How many evangelistic meetings were conducted in the past year?

10. What are the ministry goals for the current year? for next year?

11. Does the mission organization have an ongoing reporting/evaluation program which includes unannounced visits to the individual workers to verify the fruits of their ministries?

Most of us are unable to go in person and inspect the work of native missionaries. Thus we need to know that the mission organization through which the native missionary works in the West has proper systems and procedures in operation to ensure that effective ministry results from our investment. Ultimately, it is the Lord who must lead us, and He will also provide us with wisdom and discernment as we humbly seek Him.

I trust that I've been able to assist families, small groups, churches and others to gain at least some perspective on the issue. We at Gospel for Asia are ready and willing to offer you further assistance, should you have any questions or need additional information. Please feel free to call on us.

The men and women we desire to support are human. Just like us, they will sometimes make improper choices and will struggle with fleshly motives. But we must remember this: *God has called native missionaries to finish the task of world evangelism in this last hour.* So our response must be encouragement and guidance when needed rather than criticism. More than simply supporting them financially, *we must pray for them* that they will not fall prey to the many trials and temptations before them. We must resist Satan on their behalf.

We must pray also for churches, denominations and mission organizations throughout the West to recognize our brothers and sisters from developing countries as co-workers in God's great harvest.

But speaking the truth in love, [we] may grow up into him in all things, which is the head, even Christ: From whom the whole body fitly joined together and compacted by that which every joint supplieth, according to the effectual working in the measure of every part, maketh increase of the body unto the edifying of itself in love (Eph. 4:15-16).

And as God calls us to further His kingdom through supporting our brothers and sisters in the Third World, we will experience afresh what a joy and privilege it is to obey Him.

Thank you for joining in this revolution of men and women who are ready to die, if need be, to reach their own people. I pray that your desire to help reach the unreached will grow deeper in the days to come, as we approach the return of our great God and Savior Jesus Christ! May the Lord guide and direct your steps as you give of what He has given you.

Notes

[1]Calvin Kytle, *Gandhi, Soldier of Nonviolence* (New York, N.Y.: Grosset & Dunlap, 1969), pp. 102-104.

Conclusion

Today, as each second of the clock ticks by, one by one thousands of people in the Third World die and go to hell. They slip into eternity before anyone can reach them with the gospel of Jesus Christ.

What can we do about this?

In this world we can manufacture, produce or buy almost anything. But one thing we are not able to obtain, even with all the money in the world, is one additional minute of time. All we have are the twenty-four hours that are called today — the same as yesterday and tomorrow.

If there isn't anything we can do to lengthen time, should we give in to the assumption that these thousands of people are beyond our reach? No! There is something we can do — we can make better use of our time. For example, if it normally takes one month to reach a million people with the gospel, we must find a way to reach them in one day instead.

In order to do this we would need to multiply all our efforts thirty times. We would use thirty times more people, thirty times greater efficiency, thirty times more equipment and thirty times more money. In this way we would gain twenty-nine extra events instead of only one. We would improve our use of time.

What does it really take, then, to improve our use of time and reach our generation with the gospel in this decade? It takes desperate people who are gripped by urgency. The cry of their hearts is, There are only minutes left before eternity starts for millions of lost souls!

In my travels I have met a few people who share this desperation with me. I am cut deeply when I hear how casually God's people, even key leaders, talk about the lost world.

Time is short. We are not engaged in war games — this is real war.

No serious Bible student doubts that we are at a critical turning point in human history. Events and predictions that were once only the subject of idle speculation are now occurring right before our eyes.

The end of this age rushes toward us.

Since first beginning to write these pages, I have seen major changes take place in world evangelism as spiritual revival sweeps nation after nation. The world has turned upside down, providing us with many opportunities in harvest fields long denied. The events in Israel and elsewhere seem to promise the soon return of Christ.

What some might have considered merely academic arguments about strategy are taking on new urgency. The speeding events of history demand that we finish world evangelism in the most effective and efficient way possible, and as quickly as possible.

At the same time we must remember that before the Great Commission was made another command was already in effect: to love.

Hours before He made His ultimate sacrifice, Jesus told His disciples, "A new commandment I give unto you, that ye love one another; as I have loved you, that ye also love one another" (John 13:34).

The kind of love Jesus talked about goes far beyond pleasant words and occasional kind deeds. This is the love Jesus displayed when He "made himself of no reputation, and took upon him the form of a servant...and became obedient unto death" (Phil. 2:7-8).

Having the love of God in our hearts means a death sentence to our flesh. Just as Jesus gave up His will for the Father's, we give up any rights to our own plans, our own dreams.

Having the love of God in our hearts means that as we die, He is able to produce fruit through our surrendered lives (John 12:24). His love in our lives will move us to action for the lost world all around us.

Having the love of God in our hearts is the only way we can make a dramatic difference in our world for His kingdom. When His love flows through us, we will reach out to the unreached with the gospel.

God is continuing to raise up thousands of new indigenous native missionaries to complete the task in one closed nation after another. At the same time we are watching the forces of darkness mount ferocious attacks against the people of God.

Sensitive believers realize there is no doubt that Christ will soon return for His bride and that in fact we are now seeing the Holy Spirit write the last pages of church history.

Time is short. The world is at the brink of eternity. Right now we have the greatest opportunity to rise up and take the victory of the cross to the last corners of this earth.

The Lord Jesus is graciously calling a remnant to the joys of simple obedience. For those who respond, I believe there is an opportunity right now to share in the last great move of God before Christ returns.

May I encourage you — my brother, my sister — to allow God's love to overcome you and make you truly effective for His kingdom. May God give us the strength and grace to leave behind our apathy and lukewarmness and become desperate enough to "redeem the time" as He has told us to do.

It is my sincere prayer that you will be one of those who will join hands with native missionaries in this last great harvest.

Appendix

Application Questions

Evaluate the mission agencies you and your church are currently supporting:

a. Were they formed before 1939?
b. If so, have they altered their policies to include support of native missions in countries closed to Westerners?
c. On the field, is the work headed by Western or native leaders?
d. Are there indigenous churches already existing in the area?
e. If so, how does the mission agency relate to these churches?
f. Is it necessary to have a foreigner doing these tasks, or would it be possible to support a native missionary doing the same things?
g. Are the Western missionaries making disciples to replace themselves?

As you discover the answers to these questions, do you find any patterns of change in the past? Do you see any willingness to be flexible as country situations fluctuate? These are good indications that a mission agency is open to non-Western alternatives. On the other hand, if you sense an attitude of "it worked before, so it will work again" as you evaluate, this agency may need to refocus its priorities.

Evaluate the criteria for selecting the missionaries you and your church support:

a. Are there any unwritten qualifications or assumptions that are as important as the written ones?
b. Are there "secret standards" for acceptance of missionaries that are not openly acknowledged?
c. Are all your missionaries from the same church, denomination, school or association?
d. Are they all of the same race, language or nationality?
e. Are there standards that are purely cultural?
f. Do you feel they are applied equally and fairly?
g. Are they required of native missionaries as well as foreign missionaries?
h. What percentage of your missionaries are foreign to the field, and what percentage are indigenous?

Ask the Holy Spirit to search your heart and reveal if your standards have a real basis in Scripture. If you sense a distrust of indigenous missions and churches in these qualifications or an emphasis on Western importance, these standards are not biblical. Prayerfully consider how to reform these requirements according to Jesus' servant example in the New Testament.

Analyze the job description of the missionaries you and your church support according to their primary purpose. Each missionary should be able to fit his or her job description into one of three primary categories: (1) evangelism and church planting, (2) nurturing or developing existing churches or (3) other ministries. Those under the third category should be examined most carefully:

a. What percentage of support is going to social services?
b. Is the relief distributed by local churches?

c. Is the program staff Christian?
d. Has it actually helped the witness of the church in the area?
e. Are medical missionaries and others involved in human need actually able to witness?
f. Have they established churches as a result of their ministry?

If you find that the ministry of social services has become the primary goal of a mission agency rather than a secondary outcome, carefully consider whether your funds are truly being spent for evangelistic purposes.

Review the budgets of your missions projects:

a. Is most of the missions money going to support foreign workers?
b. Is it going to help support native missionaries and to purchase the tools and supplies they need to reach their own people?
c. What percentage of your missions giving goes to evangelism, church planting and evangelistic tools?

If you attempt to stay aware of current events and are sensitive to special opportunities that arise on the mission field, your involvement in missions is more than likely meeting the critical needs.

Read through recent prayer letters and annual activity reports of your missionaries:

a. How many heard the gospel as a result of their ministries in the past year?
b. How many converted to Christ and were baptized?
c. How many new churches were established?

If you find that the missionaries you support are not directly involved in or enabling and serving ministries to win souls and plant churches, consider whether these activities are justified by the Great Commission mandate of Christ — especially in light of the billions still unreached.

Examine the regions of the world where each of your missionaries is serving:

a. Is there a local, thriving body of believers nearby?
b. Could native missionaries from that local church be sent out and supported instead of a foreign missionary?

As you consider these alternatives, they will either clash or agree with your worldview of missions. If you hold to a "field perspective," you will be more concerned about how unreached people groups can best receive the gospel. If you are only concerned about how you or your church can reach the world, your worldview needs some redirection to the real issue at hand.

Evaluate your personal viewpoint and your church's policy on the role of the supernatural in evangelism:

a. Is there any attempt to explain away the occurrence of miracles and other supernatural events?
b. Ask missionaries about their experiences of the evidence of God's power on the mission field. Have they felt free to share everything that has taken place?

Prayerfully evaluate these policies in light of Jesus' ministry and that of the New Testament apostles. If you sense a resistance to the movement of the Holy Spirit, ask the Lord to open your heart to His plan for the world.

As you evaluate your standards for sending out missionaries, examine the fruit of their lives.

a. How much emphasis is put on skills and abilities, and how much on the calling of God?
b. How long has it been since any revisions were made to your policy?

If you see God-given gifts, an uncompromising obedience to His call and a willingness to stand alone for Jesus' sake, you can be assured of their authenticity. If there is an absence of these characteristics, carefully reconsider the qualifications used in sending these missionaries to the field.

If you have been stirred by the message of this book and would like to know more about the ministry of Gospel for Asia, please write or call today:

Gospel for Asia
1932 Walnut Plaza
Carrollton, TX 75006
(214) 416-0340

In Canada:
Gospel for Asia
P.O. Box 4000
Waterdown, ON LOR 2HO

OTHER BOOKS BY K.P. YOHANNAN:

The Coming Revolution in World Missions. Altamonte Springs, Fla.: Creation House, Strang Communications Company, 1986, 1989.

An exciting narrative that tells the story of how K.P. Yohannan received the vision to start Gospel for Asia and discovered the message and ministry to which God called him.

The Road to Reality. Altamonte Springs, Fla.: Creation House, Strang Communications Company, 1988.

This inspiring book is both prophetic and practical. It was written to help Christians with a world vision become more faithful disciples of Christ and disentangle themselves from the attractions of this world.